PORTFOLIO / PENGUIN

THE $1,000 CHALLENGE

Brian J. O'Connor is a syndicated columnist for *The Detroit News*. For his "Grand Experiment" series he was honored with a 2010 Best in Business award from the Society of American Business Editors and Writers and the Christopher J. Welles Memorial Prize, awarded by the Columbia University Graduate School of Journalism. He lives outside Detroit with his wife and son.

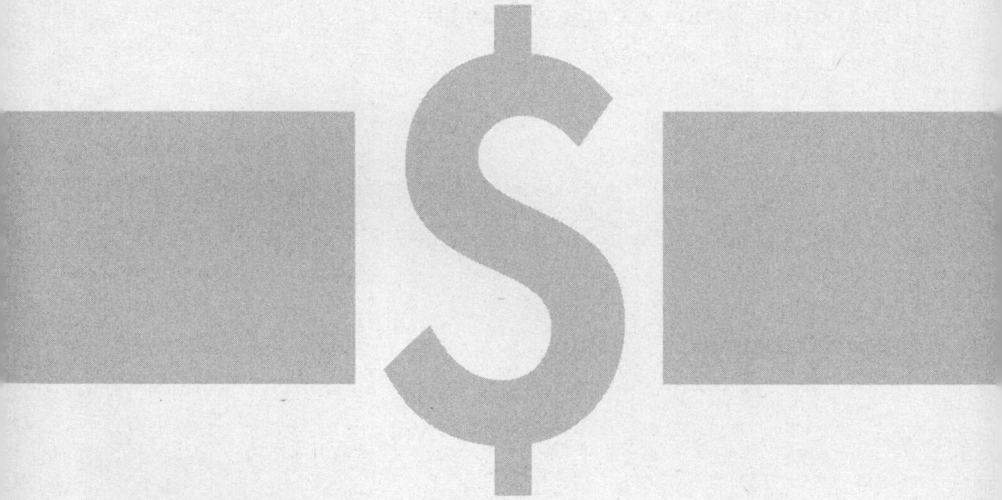

Praise for *The $1,000 Challenge*

"Who says deep digging into personal finance has to be drudgery? Brian O'Connor, aka "Mr. Funny Money," mines invaluable gold nuggets on his own personal financial experiment and leaves you smarter, empowered, and laughing all the way."
—Teri Gault, founder and CEO of TheGroceryGame.com

"O'Connor can make negotiating a lower bill with his cable company funny. This book made me laugh and cancel my unused gym membership." —Jennifer Reese, author of *Make the Bread, Buy the Butter*

"Whoever said you can't cut your way to prosperity has never read Brian J. O'Connor. Squeeze out all the wasteful spending in your household budget and you may find you're richer than you think. This book will help you recover even if the economy around you does not."
Al Lewis, columnist, MarketWatch and
The Wall Street Journal Sunday

"If the Funny Money family can find a way to save $1,000 in the middle of job furloughs, hefty special ed expenses for Li'l Money all the while helping Grandpa with his medical bills, you can, too. Mr. Funny Money, Brian O'Connor, reveals in his typical riotous style simple how-to's for getting it done. Join in the Funny Money family's adventure and you'll find yourself packing your emergency savings account faster than you could run from his recipe for roasted raccoons. *The $1,000 Challenge* is a must-read no matter how dire your financial predicament." —Julie Bandy, editor-in-chief of Bankrate.com

"Far too much personal finance writing tastes like medicine. Brian's financial advice goes down smoothly, with a generous coating of humor that helps a serious money message and a lot of practical tips slide right through. Along the way, he punctures the oft-peddled notion that paring back is easily done by trimming back a few luxuries (take that, latte police!). Saving money and trimming a budget is hard but doable work, but it's made easier with Brian's well-thought-out tips." —Daniel P. Ray, editor-in-chief of CreditCards.com

The
$1,000
Challenge

How One Family Slashed Its Budget
Without Moving Under a Bridge or
Living on Government Cheese

Brian J. O'Connor

PORTFOLIO/PENGUIN

PORTFOLIO / PENGUIN
Published by the Penguin Group
Penguin Group (USA) LLC
375 Hudson Street
New York, New York 10014

USA | Canada | UK | Ireland | Australia | New Zealand | India | South Africa | China
penguin.com
A Penguin Random House Company

First published by Portfolio / Penguin, a member of Penguin Group (USA) LLC, 2013

LIBRARY OF CONGRESS CATALOGING-IN-PUBLICATION DATA
O'Connor, Brian J., 1959–
The $1,000 challenge : how one family slashed its budget without moving under a bridge or living on government cheese / Brian J. O'Connor.
pages cm
Summary: "A funny, useful guide to saving $1,000 a month, based on the popular series in The Detroit News. With middle-class families more stretched than ever, nationally syndicated personal finance columnist Brian O'Connor decided to test his own advice about saving money. He began a ten-week experiment to cut his family's monthly expenses by $1,000—without sacrificing anything truly important. The result is a funny, savvy guide to budgeting in the real world, across ten different categories of spending. It can help families eliminate petty squabbling about money and feel better about where those hard-earned dollars are going"— Provided by publisher.
ISBN 978-1-59184-643-7 (pbk.)
1. Budgets, Personal. 2. Finance, Personal. 3. Frugality. 4. Home economics—Accounting.
5. Consumer education. I. Title. II. Title: One thousand dollar challenge.
HG179.O266 2013
332.024—dc23
2013023196

Printed in the United States of America
1 3 5 7 9 10 8 6 4 2

Set in Adobe Caslon Pro
Designed by Alissa Amell

To Jodi, Casey, and Mom

CONTENTS

INTRODUCTION

The Great Recessepression

How to Use This Very Handy and Enlightening
Book, Even If You Don't Happen to Be a
Chicken-Dancing Polish Farm Worker

Pop Quiz: How did you spend September 20?

A. Cleaning and restuffing your feathered suit for National
   Chicken Dance Day.
B. Marking the Feast of Zywie, the Polish goddess of lon-
   gevity, by not dying.
C. Marking National Farm Safety Day, also by not dying
   (only counts if you work on a farm).
D. Celebrating Constitution Week by refusing to quarter
   foreign soldiers in your home (unless they're really, really
   cute, in which case, hey, go for it).

If you did any of these things, you somehow managed to overlook
the anniversary of VR Day—Victory over Recession. It was pre-
cisely on September 20, 2010, that the economic eggheads in charge
of deciding such things declared that the worst financial downturn
since the Great Depression had officially ended more than a year

earlier. Some call it the "Great Recession," since it was much worse than other downturns we've been through, while others label it the "Lesser Depression." I say split the difference and let's call it the Great Recessepression.

Whatever we call it, marking the end of such economic wretchedness is normally the kind of auspicious occasion that would make me want to throw on a sailor suit, run to Times Square, and kiss a nurse. But not this year. The National Bureau of Economic Review may have declared the recession over years ago, but for many Americans, it's still going strong. And, much like watching the broadcast of the Oscars, it feels like it's going to last for the rest of our lives.

More than four years after the official end of the recession, more than twelve million Americans remained unemployed in the first quarter of 2013, with 40 percent of them out of work for more than six months. A third of homeowners owe more on their mortgages than their homes are worth. Real wages have fallen for the past several decades, and pay has continued to decline since the end of the recession. Credit is harder to get, student loan debt has ballooned to become a crisis, and retirees are entering their golden years with bank accounts paying nearly 0 percent interest and with nest eggs that gained little, if anything, between 2000 and 2012. Seniors owe more on their credit cards, baby boomers have seen their incomes drop by nearly 10 percent since the end of 2009, and the net worth of anyone younger than forty is either flat or lower than it was for people the same age in 1983.

I could go on (and frequently do), but the bottom line is that even with the recession ended and the economy "recovering," anyone of any age is going to need to save more, invest more, and spend less for the foreseeable future. The good news is that the best, fastest return on your effort is to find ways to cut your spending. A penny saved is a penny earned, according to Ben Franklin, but Ben lived before the income tax, plus I suspect the math part of his brain got fried by all that kite flying during lightning storms. These days a penny saved is nearly a penny-and-a-half earned before taxes. So, if you cut your spending by $100 and send that to your savings account, it's like your boss gave you a raise of $142. Even better, your savings account can't fire you and won't make you come to lame-o office parties where Tracie from accounts payable is going to make the DJ play ABBA all night.

So, you need to save, but how do you do it? You could listen to the money gurus who think we're all a bunch of shiftless yuppies blowing our money on $5 lattes and who endlessly lecture that all you need to do is cut back on life's luxuries. Well, the latte police have it wrong. Nobody is going to build up an emergency fund equal to eight months of living expenses, or create a retirement fund to last thirty years, or pay a mortgage after they lose their job by skipping the occasional trip to Starbucks. Yes, if you're broke it's foolish not to realize that the cost of one deluxe coffee can keep you in beans and rice for a week. I'm just saying that pinching every penny in your pocket is a miserable way to live, and ineffective, too, since most people can't sustain it.

Instead of worrying and scrimping, make a plan. You'll need to put together a budget, track your spending, and figure out what you're going to have to do to make ends meet and provide for your future. That takes a while. In the meantime, especially when a financial crisis hits, you need to conserve cash now. The best way is to look at your largest recurring monthly expenses and squeeze as much as you can—or at least need—out of that spending.

That's what I did as the Funny Money columnist for *The Detroit News* when the recession threatened my family—me, Mrs. Funny Money, and my boy, Funny Money Jr. I chose our family's ten biggest spending categories and aimed to cut $100 from each one. Your categories may be different from mine, but the ones in this book are pretty common. Even if yours are different, you can apply the same approach to reducing your costs.

How much you want to save, and how much you realistically *can* save, will depend on your situation. If you're in dire circumstances, you may not be able to do much more than limit the damage. If that seems like your case, talk to a certified debt counselor or even a bankruptcy expert right away. But even then, you're going to need cash, so keep cutting. For those of us who aren't falling over the edge, saving more and spending less is the best cushion from the ravages of the ongoing troubled economy and can allow you to make up lost ground in reaching your financial goals, whether that's buying a new powerboat or just knowing that, in retirement, instead of generic Metamucil you'll be able to afford the real thing.

Armed mostly with this book, you can weed out the unnecessary spending that exists in any budget, whether it's the result of being less than systematic in your approach to grocery shopping or just lazy in looking over your bills. In some cases I cut more than $100 a month from our budget with only a few phone calls. In others you'll need to do some extensive comparison shopping. Either way, each dollar you save is not only more than the dollar you earn, but it also represents real savings you can enjoy month after month.

Beyond cutting costs, you should look for other ways to put your financial house in order. The two most important things you can do are to build and maintain an emergency fund and avoid adding new debt while systematically paying down your past borrowing at a reasonable rate that lets you live the rest of your life.

I've organized this book starting with the easiest savings you can find, then moving on to more difficult choices as you either need or want to. It's organized according to three approaches:

Freeing up cash

If you're following this approach, you're basically okay but your financial picture could be better. You're working, and your spouse is working or not, as you both have agreed, but you need more cash to meet your goals. You're managing to pay your monthly bills but sometimes end up putting things on credit cards and not paying them off each month. Maybe you need to bolster your emergency fund, save for a vacation or other goal, boost your retirement savings, or pay down debt.

Making ends meet

This means most of your bills get paid each month, but it's a stretch. You're working, but perhaps your spouse got laid off from his or her part-time job, or you had your hours cut back at work, or you're underemployed, working part-time when you need a full-time gig, or making less than you need. You make minimum payments on your credit cards, and then just barely. Your emergency fund is minuscule if you have one at all, and any unexpected bills come at the expense of other things. You need to create some breathing room in your monthly cash flow and build up your emergency fund. Then you can start to think about paying off debt and saving for retirement and other goals.

Pinching pennies so hard that Lincoln gets a headache

You don't have enough to pay the bills, you're burning through your savings (if you ever had any), the credit cards will soon be maxed out, and you're focused simply on surviving. You or your spouse has been laid off from a full-time job, and the family income has been cut by half or more. Your focus is on keeping food on the table, a roof over your head, and the power, gas, and water running until you can get some new income or find another way out.

You may not be able to make much progress in some categories, but don't let that stop you. Set a specific goal and strive to make enough cuts to hit it. You don't need to set yourself a $1,000 challenge—I chose $1,000 because it made a nice headline—but do make it some sort of challenge. You'll be surprised at how much the satisfaction of hitting your goal offsets the minor inconvenience of shopping off the rack of day-old bread.

That way, we can all celebrate next September 20 in our own personal Victory over Recessepression Day. Unless, of course, you're a Polish farm worker. In that case, stay safe, take the day off, and invite a cute foreign soldier to go chicken dancing.

$ 1

The Motown Breakdown

In Which Your Author Discovers That While
He *Can* Go Home Again, It Might Not Have
Been the Shrewdest Financial Move

Before we go any further, I want to make it clear that I never have eaten raccoon. Although I am not making any promises, especially if the varmints don't stay away from the tomato plants.

Let me explain.

As the award-winning personal finance columnist for *The Detroit News*, it's hard to admit that in March 2005, shortly before the recession hit, I'd made the kind of shrewd money move that defines any good personal finance writer: a massive, idiotic, potentially life-ruining financial blunder.

I moved to Detroit. To take a newspaper job.

Now, before you mock me, consider that I had the very best of reasons. For three years I'd been an unemployed, stay-at-home, freelancing, job-hunting dad who needed a break—and a paycheck—after converting my cordless drill into the world's most powerful baby-bottle brush.

Besides, all the jobs as buggy-whip makers were taken in Mogadishu.

1

At the beginning, luck seemed on my side as I started writing the column for *The Detroit News* that's now syndicated as Funny Money. The move back to my hometown would also allow my son to spend time with his grandmother, who was yearning to spoil the boy with the same peanut butter cookies that had been a constant in my childhood. I had explained to her, several times, that she, being retired, was supposed to move to Florida to be near her grandson, not the other way around. But you can't get old people out of Michigan with dynamite. Whenever I run into another middle-aged guy who has just moved back to my mitten-shaped home state, I simply ask, "Grandparents, right?" and he nods knowingly.

My wife, an extremely shy woman known in print only as Mrs. Funny Money, agreed to move and leave behind our idyllic life of giant killer pythons in the Everglades, a lawn the texture of a Brillo Pad, and the annual invasions of sea lice and wizened snowbirds in rental cars (sea lice are terrible drivers). Mrs. Funny Money gave up her job of twenty years, we scraped the "Welcome to Florida—Thanks for Not Shooting!" bumper stickers off our cars, and we headed north to the land of idle smokestacks, black ice, and potholes with my blond-haired, then-four-year old boy, Funny Money Jr. or, as I call him, Li'l Money ('cuz that's all he leaves us).

We'd made a tidy profit on our home in south Florida, selling near the peak of the mortgage mania. On the day before our closing, a woman rang our front doorbell and, without setting foot into the house, offered me $10,000 over our best offer.

This is where a savvy personal finance expert should have realized that the mortgage madness had overheated to the point where it would soon melt into a burned, galled disaster. The smart move would have been to take the money, bury it in a Mason jar, and pitch a tent at the nearest state campground until the housing market tumbled to its inevitable bottom. Instead, I counseled the prospective buyer on my doorstep to keep shopping but consider adjusting her medication.

The fast sale of our house left us with no debt, plenty of savings, and a tidy wad of cash to put down on a new home in the Great Lakes State. The plan was for my chain-smoking, ex-farmer, former-Marine father-in-law, Verne, to live half the year with us and half in his Florida condo.

Hoping to channel the extremely independent and opinionated Grandpa Verne and our energetic preschooler into neutral corners, we settled on a four-bedroom trilevel in Sylvan Lake, a lakeside suburb close to my mom. Despite Michigan's already shrinking economy, real estate prices had climbed there, too, so we paid more than I'd planned. Then we paid even more, since the lunatic owner pulled the house off the market in the middle of January, the day before our inspection. Still, I bear her no ill will and even wish her long life. With incurable diarrhea.

Salvation arrived in the form of a lovely five-bedroom bilevel right down the street from Lunatic Diarrhea Lady (location, location, location!). In early March, Mrs. Funny Money and Li'l Money arrived. Mrs. Funny Money hadn't seen the house, but she instantly cooed her one-word approval: "Perfect." I have been blissfully happy only a few times in my life: the night I proposed, the day Li'l Money was born, the first time I got the word "poop" into a newspaper column. But the moment that my wife approved of moving into a home she'd never laid eyes on beats them all.

Together again, we were happy in our new home. My mom was happy to have us nearby, and Grandpa Verne was happy to avoid the Michigan snow by staying in Florida until the summer. I had a new job at a major paper, and the editors already wanted to hire my wife. But she was in no hurry. We had saved enough money for her to spend a year getting us settled and even had a few bucks more set aside to spruce up the house. Sure, we had spent $60,000 more than we had planned on the house, but in a year she'd be working again. In the meantime, I would hang on to some of my freelance clients for extra cash.

During the first night in our new home, an inch of snow fell, and I happily shoveled it away the next morning. Soon, I knew, the tulips would be pushing up in our new garden, and a Michigan summer would bring lazy days at the lake, just a few blocks away.

Perfect, right?

At this point you're probably wondering, "Is this where the raccoons come in? Because I believe I was promised raccoons." No, the raccoons didn't show up until the recession, which was two years away—for the rest of the country.

After the recession of 2001, following the crash of the Internet-fueled tech bubble and the terrorist attacks of September 11, most Americans switched from spending their spurious tech-bubble riches to tapping their equally bogus home equity, and by the mid-2000s had turned their houses into little more than dry-walled ATMs. Things were very different in Michigan by the time I moved there in the spring of 2005. The tech boom of the 1990s had been old Detroit's last hurrah, when the state jobless rate actually dropped below the U.S. average as Internet entrepreneurs loaded up on Escalades and other fancy rides. Stock in General Motors soared to $94.62 a share, and shares of Ford Motor Company hit $64.77.

The state economy during the mortgage boom was very different. Even though Motown sold a lot of pickups to contractors, Michigan was already well into a decade-long one-state recession that saw the loss of more than 800,000 jobs between 2001 and 2011. Even as the U.S. jobless rate declined, Michigan's unemployment rolls kept rising. When I closed on my new Michigan home in 2005, the state's jobless rate had been worse than the U.S. average for forty months and had been more than one full point higher than the rest of the country for more than two years. By the time the Great Recession hit in December 2007, the U.S. jobless rate was 5 percent—but Michigan was already at 7.2 percent.

By September 2007, the worst, crappiest, most dishonest home loans, mostly made to unwitting subprime borrowers who never should have qualified, started going bad because, in a sane world, you cannot finance a $150,000 loan with a $300 monthly payment. The big lenders behind this dreck headed for bankruptcy, but the stock market soared undaunted on a wave of ever-rising home values. Between April 2, 2007, when New Century Financial, one of the country's largest subprime mortgage lenders, filed for bankruptcy protection, and October 9, 2007, the Dow Jones Industrial Average soared to 14,165, a record high that the blue-chip index wouldn't see again for more than five years.

Car buyers, however, got nervous. The domestic auto industry lost nearly one million in sales between 2005 and 2007, even as national employment was still improving. When the boom peaked in 2007, annual light vehicle sales in North America dropped from 17 million the year before to 16.5 million. When you live in Michigan and this is your state's major industry, that's a big problem, kind of like shark attacks on Florida tourists or a hooker shortage in Vegas. As the mortgage bubble burst, car sales fell by another three million units in just twelve months, to a devastating 10.6 million vehicle sales by the end of 2009.

Of course, if the car guys needed to feel better, they just looked at the decline of the newspapers that were chronicling their misfortune. At least, the automakers thought, nobody can drive to work on Google. Whereas the Internet was clearly turning newspapers into the next Yugo.

No one saw any of it coming, least of all me as I watched the movers pull away from my new house, unaware that Michigan's Big Mitten was slowly and surely unraveling around its newest residents.

Soon my paper was sold and cutbacks started as the automakers slid toward bankruptcy.

Things didn't get any easier on the home front, either.

My son, Li'l Money, could also be nicknamed Li'l Talker because of a severe language delay. He's been diagnosed as a late talker, a bright, engaging child with a mind that, for whatever reason, processes language less like a computer and more like a Cuisinart. His speech development will catch up eventually—but only with a lot of help.

In Florida this wasn't an issue because federal programs covered the cost of private speech therapy for preschoolers. After he turned four, and just before we relocated, he had moved into an excellent special education preschool program. In Michigan, we'd soon discover, the schools wouldn't be nearly as accommodating.

Our assigned district had a lousy program for Li'l Money, so we cobbled together a mix of private speech therapy, a special kindergarten, day care, and consultations with pricey out-of-town specialists. We moved the boy to a second school district, but we still needed the help of a $190-an-hour special education attorney to get the services he needed. It was all expensive, and none of it was covered by health insurance.

My son's three speech programs made it impossible for my wife to return to work. Whatever time she didn't spend driving our boy around found her back in Florida, tending to Grandpa Verne, who, suddenly stricken with cancer, never spent more than a week living with us. We fronted thousands of dollars a month for his care as we waited for his veteran benefits to kick in.

Then came the recession. Even though our son was now in school full-time, the crippled economy locked my wife out of a job despite her impressive résumé. Next, an ominously thin letter arrived from the bank, freezing our home equity line as plummeting home values wiped out our equity and down payment. The newspaper instituted unpaid furloughs and salary cuts, while my freelance work dried up and our credit card balances began to swell.

I knew I wasn't alone and that many others had it much, much worse. In fact, the crisis made my personal finance column more sought after than ever, as readers looked for tips on cutting their debts and shoring up their investments. I was busier than a priest on the day after Mardi Gras, basking, for a while, in my status as a personal finance expert as the economy cratered.

Then I heard about the raccoons.

Right there on the front page of *The Detroit News* one of my colleagues found a downtown hunter who raised cash by harvesting raccoons. Showing the entrepreneurial genius native to the birthplace of both the Ford Pinto and the AMC Pacer, this urban huntsman offered raccoon roasts for $12. His sales pitch? "Tastes like mutton."

The news that people were putting raccoon on the menu made me wonder how much real help I gave my readers. After decades writing about personal finance, I felt like a fraud. Yes, I was good at outlining retirement strategies and tax moves. And though it *felt* like we were fairly frugal at home, my family's balance sheet was suddenly less than reassuring. I worried whether it would be enough if I suggested taking steaks and chops off the family menu and substituting cheap selections, like mutton. ("Tastes like raccoon.")

Sure, it was easy to help people nibble around the edges of their spending to free up a couple hundred bucks a month for retirement or to pay down the Visa bill. That advice was fine for the good times. But what about when the family finances took a real hit? Was I giving my readers the kind of help they needed to get through the tough times, or would they be better off looking up the vermin-selling coot downtown? I had visions of affluent Bloomfield Hills matrons knocking at the door of a ramshackle house down past the old cement factory, dubiously sniffing, "Is the possum fresh today?"

And so I found myself in the office of my editors, proposing "The Grand Experiment" (aka The $1,000 Challenge), a series of columns in which I'd try to cut $100 a week out of my family's monthly spending for ten weeks in an attempt to save $1,000—an even grand. They assumed I already did all of this money-saving stuff and peered at me as if it were suddenly apparent that they'd hired the Milli Vanilli of personal finance writers.

"Well, sure," I told them, "I do all of it . . . or at least some of it, ha-ha. But, you know, there's always room to save more and . . ."

I quickly backed out of the office as soon as I heard someone say "yes." I vowed to keep the columns short, since I knew the paper was trying to cut back on its newsprint budget. Probably, I thought, saving space so we could start printing recipes for raccoon.

My first step was to set the rules to guide me through the project. The bedrock principle, the prime directive of the experiment, was simple: save a lot of money so I don't look like a fool.

The others rules were also simple. First, my focus would be on cutting immediate spending so that any cash a family had would last as long as possible. The second was to avoid spending money to save money, which cut out things like putting a few thousand bucks into a solar water heater in hopes that the gizmo might generate enough savings to pay for itself sometime during, say, Malia Obama's second term.

My next rule was to zero in on recurring monthly expenses. Sure, it's great to find a sale that knocks $40 off a new set of tires, but that only saves you $40 once every few years. Change your long-distance plan to save $5 a month and you'll be ahead $60 a year every year from now on. After three years that's $180, which means those next two radials are free.

Finally, to get the biggest bunch of bucks from my budgeting bang, I decided to concentrate on our ten largest spending categories. Now I just had to figure out what those were.

I'd set up a basic budget when we moved back to Michigan and thought I had a rather comprehensive approach using Quicken to track our cash flow (or, more accurately, our cash ebb). But I'd left the whole thing on automatic pilot, using it mostly at tax time to dig up deductions. When it came time to compile our year-to-date spending, I was facing the financial equivalent of a garden that hadn't been weeded in three years. Worse, Quicken had gone haywire. Drug store purchases were in four categories, our tax preparer was listed as "Baby-sitter" (which, if you asked her, wasn't all that far from the truth), and every purchase at the corner market wound up listed under "Avis Rent A Car." Yes, according to Quicken, someone at our house was renting a car three times a month. But at least whoever it was got a good deal: the exact same price as a six-pack.

My solution arrived in the form of Robin Thompson of Budget Wise Consulting in Sterling Heights. Robin is a former General Motors engineer with a master's degree in mathematics. Now she's a very practical personal finance expert who walks people through the process of getting a handle on their money. The problem, Robin said, wasn't with the computer program, but with me.

"Software is great for tracking expenditures, but not for making course corrections during the month," she told me. "By the time you look it over, you're looking in the rearview mirror."

Robin sat down with me to go over the basics of a good, functional budget. I already had the first step nailed: setting a specific financial goal. Otherwise, trying to save money for its own sake doesn't work. Deciding "I want to go to Paris sometime" is too vague to provide the right motivation, and it lacks the specificity necessary to make a real plan and chart your progress.

"You need to say, 'I plan to save $1,800 for a vacation next year by saving $150 from my paycheck each month,'" Robin says. "I tell my clients, 'Remember: a goal is just a dream with a deadline and a dollar sign.'"

The second step for good budgeting is to dig out your big expenses that show up only once or twice a year, such as insurance premiums, holiday gifts, and other bills that blow up your budget. Include how much you spent on car or home repairs last year and other unplanned expenses. Robin advises adding them all up, dividing by twelve, and having that amount automatically saved to a separate account. When one of those bills comes, transfer the money to your checking account to pay it. "Treat it just like an escrow account," Robin says.

Step three is where most folks start when they try to come up with a budget, which is all the mundane monthly expenses, from gas and groceries to the water and electric bills. One vital expense that too many people overlook is saving for retirement or—if you don't already have one—an emergency fund.

Having any kind of emergency fund will change your relationship with money and even yourself, no matter how you save for it and how long it takes. If you're starting at $0, aim to get two weeks of take-home pay saved, or at least $500 to $1,000 as a bare minimum. At the start of the recession, our emergency fund was a godsend. When it dwindled as the downturn worsened, I slept a lot worse at night. If you want to ponder just how valuable a wad of cash can be in a crisis, ask yourself this: How would that big trial have turned out for O. J. Simpson if he'd used a public defender?

As Robin told me, "You need to pay yourself first and pay that off the top of your paycheck, not the bottom," she says. "You are your most important expense. You need to look at yourself as one of your bills."

If you need a financial mantra, there it is: "I'm as important as the sewer bill."

The envelopes, please

Another tip from Robin was to control spending wherever possible by using "the envelope system," which has worked great for me. This is a budgeting approach I heard about from my parents, who used it as newlyweds back in the 1940s.

The classic approach is to cash your paycheck, then divide all your money into your budgeted amounts for each pay period and distribute the greenbacks into separate envelopes for each spending category, such as $150 for groceries, $60 for utilities, $125 for this week's part of the rent, and so on. When the cash is gone, it's gone, and you're done spending in that category until the next paycheck comes. Or, you can take cash from another envelope by cutting your spending in that category. Either way, the system keeps your spending in check because, if you don't resort to using credit, you can never spend more than the cash you've got on hand.

These days, it's hard to pay the mortgage or college savings plan with cash, and it can be challenging for two adults with debit cards, checkbooks, and jobs to coordinate cash purchases, but the envelope system works fine for any discretionary spending, such as lunches, entertainment, and so on, with money set aside for things like the car payment staying untouched in your bank account. There's an online version for budgeting your expenses, mvelopes.com, too. The idea is that instead of focusing on where your money went, you're planning where it goes and seeing the immediate effect of your financial decisions. If you have $150 in your envelope for entertainment and take $100 for a nice dinner out, you know that the remaining $50 has to last until next payday.

The only step I added to Robin's advice was to create a monthly cash-flow calendar that tracks when automated payments are made from our checking account, such as car and house payments and the boy's prepaid college tuition plan. Your monthly budget may add up to the penny, but if big charges such as student loan and mortgage payments occur in the same pay period, you could run short and end up bouncing checks or putting your rent on a credit card. Plotting your monthly spending and deposits by day, along with recurring expenses, such as each week's gas and lunch money, gives a complete picture of your monthly cash flow.

With all that done, you add your savings goal to your monthly expenses, plus your allotment for recurring nonmonthly charges, and there's your budget. Of course, that's more money than you actually make, so go back and adjust.

In the rare case that you have any leftover money, add it to your emergency fund, put it in your retirement savings, or use it to pay down debt. With "extra" cash sloshing around in your budget, you're tempted to use it to justify overspending, then forget, splurge again, and, at the end of the month, find yourself short on cash or long on the Visa bill, even though you started out with "extra" money.

Now, I know the word "budget" is a repulsive, ugly-sounding term that suggests only deprivation, misery, and suffering, like hearing someone say "diet," "joint session of Congress," or "a new motion picture from Adam Sandler!" But my budget-cutting project—ten weeks, a thousand bucks—perfectly nailed Robin's first requirement. It was a specific goal and it had a definite deadline, not to mention the consequences of looking like a total chump if I missed my goal.

So I buckled down and starting sorting out my old bank statements. Maybe, I thought, "budget" really isn't a four-letter word. (Of course, the fact that it's six explains how I got into trouble in the first place.) Nonetheless, I was on a mission to cut my family's spending by $1,000 a month, and there was no way I was going swallow my pride—even if I ended up swallowing raccoon.

2

Transportation

My Initial Cost-Cutting Is Driven to Failure,
but at Least My (T)Rusty '95 Roadmaster
Estate Wagon Gets Me There in Style

After two upgrades and four hours on tech support, I finally got my financial tracking software working. I've used Quicken since the old Windows 3.1 days, when men were men and thirteen-inch monochrome monitors ruled. I loved it then, but now it's a bulky, complicated, expensive memory hog. Many people love the online budgeting and expense-tracking site Mint.com, which I find clunky and limited (plus it's owned by the Quicken folks), but if it works for you, fine. There are several other options out there that I haven't yet been able to test, so if you find a good one, let me know. Until then, I'm grudgingly sticking with Quicken, which is the same attitude I take toward the Democratic Party.

Despite the hassle, I finally had my top ten family spending categories. Amazingly, the list didn't include long-distance phone charges to Quicken's tech support.

Our big spending mostly fell along the lines that you'd expect—housing, cars, food, and so on. To get my list, I simply divided all our monthly expenses into categories, ranging from housing to entertainment to gas and so on. Then I totaled each category for the past twelve months and picked the ten that were costing us the most. The surprise on the list was life insurance, which seemed like an awful lot of money to invest each month in my own demise.

The results were:

- **Transportation**
- **Miscellaneous**
- **Utilities**
- **Offspring**
- **Child care**
- **Personal spending**
- **Entertainment**
- **Insurance**
- **Groceries**
- **Housing**

That's in no particular arrangement other than the order in which I wound up tackling them in my newspaper columns. Housing—including mortgage principal and interest, property taxes, insurance, and repairs—was easily the biggest category. The thirty-year loan on our house was at 5.5 percent interest, and rates had dropped. I was betting that refinancing the loan would easily save me more than $100 right there, but the new, more complicated mortgage application rules meant that it would take several weeks, including arranging an independent third-party appraisal. I scheduled the housing category to run last in the series, figuring that making it my anchorman in this financial tug-of-war would result in a slam dunk, home run, touchdown, triple-word-score, or any other sports metaphors I could mix and mangle.

With housing on the back burner, I decided to tackle the auto expense category in my first "Grand Experiment" column. Between the cost of the vehicles, gas, maintenance, and insurance, I was sure I could dig out $100 of savings per month. After all, according to the Bureau of Labor Statistics, transportation is the second-largest expense for Americans, and it's easy to see why: according to TrueCar.com, in November 2012 the average price of a new car was $30,832, and that doesn't include tax, title, and other dealer charges. Even with 10 percent down and a car loan at a low rate of 3 percent, financing that cost over four years gives you a monthly payment of $704. Plus you need to either put up cash for the tax, title, license, and other dealer charges or roll them into the loan and drive your payment even higher. Carrying that kind of payment translates to more than $12,000 a year before taxes, or nearly one-quarter of the U.S. median family income.

Unfortunately, vehicle cost offered absolutely no savings in my case because I didn't have a big payment on a shiny new set of wheels. Despite being born and bred in Motown, I've never owned a new car. Maybe I'm cursed because my parents brought me home from the hospital in a '47 DeSoto. Mrs. Funny Money is less keen on used vehicles, having been scarred by a 1976 Volkswagen camper I purchased after we were married. To this day, she churlishly argues that, regardless of how nifty anyone thinks a built-in propane stove might be, any vehicle that needs to be towed to the campsite fails to qualify as a "camper."

Since then, she's insisted that she, at least, drive a new car, which we buy, pay off, and drive to death. By the time I started my budget-cutting experiment, Mrs. Funny Money was driving a dependable '97 Honda Accord we were getting ready to replace. Meanwhile, I've retained my knack for picking cars that make for handy landmarks when giving directions to our home. "You can't miss it," I say. "It's the house with the green MG/orange Citroën/surplus East German Mungo troop transport."

I'd toned down my taste for exotic and useless vehicles after fatherhood, and by the time we moved to Detroit I was driving the perfect family hauler: a 1995 Buick Roadmaster Estate Wagon. Outfitted with the same boisterous V-8 as that year's Corvette, my Roadmaster is eighteen feet of hulking, vinyl wood–veneered Detroit badassery masquerading under a cloak of dull suburban sensibility. While some may deride the Roadmaster as oversized, square, or, as certain females in my house scoff, looking "like a farm car," let me make one point: if Willard "Mittens" Romney had owned this car, he'd have had so much room that he never would have had to strap that Irish setter to the roof, and he (Mittens) would be president today.

Vehicle cost

Your best bet in lowering the cost of your car payment is to keep your payments low to begin with, by saving for a down payment, buying what you can afford, paying the loan off quickly, and performing regular maintenance and repairs so that your car lasts. I'll talk about a good way to do that at the end of this chapter, but for now let's focus on savings.

Once you're in a financial pinch, there's not a lot you can do to lower the cost of a car loan, but the few options available can put a significant amount of money back in your budget. Some of these alternatives aren't all that convenient, but they can get you through a crisis.

Freeing up cash

If you've got a car payment, look at lowering your cost. If the interest rate on your loan is high, such as you'd get from a "buy-here, pay-here" lot or though dealer financing if you had bad credit, visit a credit union and ask about refinancing your loan.

At *The Detroit News* I used to write a feature called "Money Makeover," and one of my subjects was a young guy who'd started out with an affordable car lease after graduation, only to burn through his mileage allotment before the lease was up. If he kept driving the car, he faced paying excess mileage charges. Instead, he rolled the remainder of the lease into a new loan on a pickup truck, and by the time a certified financial planner and I looked over his finances, the kid was losing a significant chunk of his paycheck to a car payment of about $600 a month. I suggested he try refinancing through a credit union where his brother was a member. I was thrilled when he called two weeks later and told me he'd cut the payment down to less than $400 a month with a new, lower-rate credit union car loan. The savings amounted to $210 a month, or more than $2,500 a year.

Just about anyone can join a community credit union, and others are extremely open. Got a brother in the Coast Guard? You can join the Navy Federal Credit Union. My brother doesn't guard America's borders, but he molds our nation's young minds, so I can join his teachers' credit union. Before you join, shop around. My *Detroit News* credit union matches loan rates at any other credit union I could join. So, when we replaced Mrs. Funny Money's Honda with a more Motown-appropriate Mercury, I found a new-member special of 2.99 percent on car loans at a competing credit union, and my credit union matched it.

If you owe more than your car is worth, refinancing the loan may not be possible. You can look to trade the car in for something cheaper, but this could leave you with an unpaid balance on the original loan. Rolling the debt from the old loan into a new car payment is risky, though some dealers will do it. But it means you're overpaying for your new, cheaper ride, you're still going to owe more than the new vehicle is worth, and you're leaving your budget stretched. Plus, since that "new" car is probably a very used one, you run the risk of having that car break down, causing you to spend more money to keep it going.

It's easier to roll over a lease into a new lease or loan, but you run the same risk of adding the balance of what's owed on your old lease to a new one. A better option is getting someone to take over your lease through one of the online services that matches people who need a cheap car with lease customers who need to get out of their agreement. Two of the bigger ones are LeaseTrader.com and Swapalease.com. First check that your finance company will allow a lease transfer and that you won't have any liability for the car or the balance once the lease is transferred.

Your best bet may be simply to suck it up for now and continue making payments until the car is worth more than you owe, at which point you can sell it and buy something cheaper or refinance. But first check what your car is worth. Used car values have jumped in the past four years, and your current ride may be worth more than you think, which means you can sell it and get something less expensive. If it's a leased car and it's worth more than you owe, you don't have to return it to the dealer. Instead, you can sell it to any dealer or private party, or trade it in for a new ride. (You can find a good outline of everything involved from Edmunds.com.)[1]

Making ends meet

People struggling just to get by should look at refinancing, or selling and buying something cheaper first. After that, you'll need to get creative. Maybe a relative or friend is willing to buy your car by taking over the payments. Be careful to set up any such deal as a real business transaction with a written agreement that spells out how much and when they'll pay, who's responsible for maintenance and repairs, what happens if the car breaks down, and what happens if the other party can't pay you. You'll also need to arrange insurance in both of your names.

If you lease, one of the lease-swapping sites can help you set up a deal with a friend or relative to take over the lease. If you're running up against extra mileage charges, your options include swapping cars with someone who drives less so that you'll have lower mileage charges when you turn in the car, or you might have to park it until the lease is up and find other transportation.

If the gap between what you owe on the car and what it's worth isn't too big, you can consider paying off the difference so you can sell or trade the car for something cheaper, or refinance to a less expensive loan. That's easy enough if you've got some cash on hand or you can save up, but don't drain your emergency fund and expose yourself to more financial risk. We're trying to free up cash here, not blow it all by wheeling and dealing on used cars.

Of course, if the car is paid off and you can find a way to live without it, even for a while, just sell it. You'll get a one-time infusion of cash and eliminate all the overhead that the car entails—gas, repairs, insurance, tolls, and even buying new pine-tree air fresheners. After you've paid down your debt or saved up for your goal, you can go out and find a car that fits your budget.

Pinching pennies so hard that Lincoln gets a headache

All the options we've looked at so far focus on how to lower your payment without damaging your credit or leaving yourself stuck with an unpaid balance on an old loan or lease that will continue to cost you. If you're in dire straits, though, you need to do whatever it takes to preserve whatever cash and income you have while covering the basic necessities.

If none of the options discussed above work for you and you're stuck with a payment or lease you know you can't keep making, talk to your lender. If you're lucky, you might be able to get a temporary reprieve or negotiate new financing, which will likely cost more in the long run but could lower your payments now and allow you to keep driving the car. If you can't make a deal, your best bet is to surrender the car. Your credit will take a hit and you'll owe the balance, plus any penalties if you ended a lease early or if the loan has an early payoff penalty. It's hard, but if you're going to end up losing the vehicle anyway, it's better to give it up on your terms rather than wait for the repo man to grab it. Plus, the lender will hit you with the repo costs on top of your unpaid loan balance.

If a lender-dealer offers to renegotiate your loan and put you into a cheaper car, be careful. Check out any replacement vehicle thoroughly. You don't want to end up carrying your old loan plus a new loan on a car that falls apart in six months, leaving you with more debt on two cars and no actual transportation. Before defaulting on a car loan or lease, though, work through the other savings strategies in this chapter and the rest of the book to see whether you can find other costs you can cut to free up cash for your car payment.

How to buy a car

The best way to keep a car payment from crashing your budget is to keep your initial payments affordable. The usual options are to save more or spend less, but a third strategy accomplishes both. The idea is to purchase a car that you can pay off in three years, then bank what you used to spend on your car payment as you drive the vehicle as long as you can. Do that twice, and you'll have lots of cash to put down on a car the third time around.

For example, a $400 payment at 3 percent means you can finance

$13,750 for a car today. That's probably a 2007 model, which you drive for five years. It's paid off after three and you save for two, socking away $9,600 toward a replacement. By then interest rates should have increased, so let's say you finance the second car at 7 percent, borrowing $13,000. Add your $9,600 in savings and that's $22,600 to spend—and you're putting 44 percent down in cash.

More money means a better car, and let's say that gives you four years to drive and save after paying it off once again in three years. By then you've saved $19,200 and you're paying well more than half the cost of your new car in cash—or all the cost of a good used car—plus you've kept your payment steady at $400 for the last twelve years.

If you can drive your cars longer between buying replacement vehicles, you can accumulate even more cash and get to the point of buying a car for all cash sooner. (You can really stretch your car cash by purchasing well-cared-for, two-year-old used vehicles instead of new ones. You can find a good selection of those models coming off leases, often with the remainder of the warranty or certified by the dealer.) Plus, I haven't factored in any additional cash or reduced payment you'll get on your trade-in, since that will vary according to how well you take care of the car and whether you drive that puppy straight into the ground.

Yeah, sometimes you have to put up with handling repairs or driving with a noisy muffler until you can get to the repair shop, but the savings should make that sound like music to your ears.

Insurance

Unfortunately for the sake of finding savings, both the Roadmaster and Mrs. Funny Money's Honda were paid off. With no car payment to cut, I looked elsewhere for savings. That left maintenance, insurance, and gas as my remaining savings targets. Thanks to a trustworthy mechanic, I couldn't find any unnecessary repairs on either car. In dire straits, I could have started changing my own oil, but that wouldn't net even $20 a month. Plus, I'd probably procrastinate and end up seizing the engine.

When it came to insurance, I already had a pretty good deal. The one bright spot I could find was that switching from monthly billing to paying my premium every six months would save $54.87 on a six-month renewal. That cut my car cost by a whopping $6.31 a month.

The only other way to trim my auto insurance would be to dump the comprehensive (fire, vandalism, theft, and other noncollision damage) and collision coverage on the two cars, which would save about $600 a year. It's a good idea, except for the Roadmaster's nickname, "The Deerslayer."

That's not because I'm a fan of *The Last of the Mohicans*, but because in one fourteen-month period, the car sent two deer to the not-so-happy hunting grounds in the sky. I know that hunters seek every advantage when stalking the wily whitetail: high-tech camouflage, state-of-the-art rifle optics, and even a half pint of deer urine, which, I suppose, hunters dab behind each ear for that "fresh from the latrine" aroma no animal can resist.

But when it comes to fatal attraction, deer tinkle has nothing on my General Motors V-8. Thanks to my collision coverage, though, I haven't put out a penny to fix the car, saving me $2,000 in deductible payments. The insurance company called the accidents "acts of God," and, since the first one happened in the October rutting season, I'll admit that there must have been an act of some kind on the mind of that deer.

Finding savings in your insurance is easier than cutting your car payment. Just make sure that if you reduce your coverage you don't take on more risk that could leave you in worse financial shape. Remember, after all, that there are eleven million car crashes each year.

Freeing up cash

If you've got savings, your first step is to raise your deductible on all your insurance policies. Typically, a policy starts with a $500 deductible, but raising it to $1,000 will lower your payment. Also, if you're comfortable enough to afford it, paying your premium annually or every six months also will trim your bill.

Your next step is to shop around. Even if you're as thrilled with your insurance agent as I am with mine, companies introduce new deals and discounts all the time, and different agents may have different approaches to help you lower your premium. This also helps you identify changes that need to be made on your policy, such as a teen driver who's moved out of the house or a car that's aged to the point where it no longer requires comp and collision.

While you're shopping, aggressively quiz the sales reps about every possible combination of coverage and discounts possible. You can get a discount for not having an accident, for driving (or not driving) a certain type of car, for being a member of AAA, or being a dues-paying member of the Crippled Canary Society. My best discount on auto insurance comes from combining my home and auto insurance with the same agent. In fact, you can get discounts you don't really want. My agent automatically applied an over-fifty discount for wizened, drooling old fogies a few months before I hit my fifth decade, even as I tried to ignore that dubious milestone.

You can get additional insurance reductions for making more effort, such as taking a defensive driving course or installing a car alarm. First check how much this is going to save you, because there's a cost to taking a course or adding electronics. If the investment doesn't pay for itself right away, it violates our $1,000 Challenge rule that we don't pay out money now to eventually save a little money on some distant break-even point years down the road.

Shop around for insurance every couple of years just to make sure you are getting the right coverage at the best possible price.

Making ends meet

Check your policy for add-ons and coverage that you can live without or may not need anymore. Coverage that replaces a broken windshield may be something you can cut. Instead, you can "self-insure" by having savings and an emergency fund on hand to fix or replace a cracked window. And since your car has aged since you first took out the policy, it might be time to drop your collision and comprehensive coverage. The standard rule of thumb is that if you car is worth less than ten times the amount you pay for annual comp and collision, it's time to cancel the coverage, which can account for up to 40 percent of your insurance bill. If you do cancel collision and comp, direct at least some of the money into a savings account to fix the car if you have a serious accident or, since that vehicle is getting pretty old, to eventually replace it.

If you've been pinched to pay all your bills at times, chances are that you paid some of them late. If those payments were more than thirty days past due, your credit has likely taken a hit, which has lowered your credit score, that magical number that's grown to be almost important as your IQ or dress size. A bad credit score can send your insurance premium shooting sky-high faster than having an actual accident that requires a payout from the insurance company.

What does paying your Visa bill on time have to do with your ability to drive to work without running red lights and plowing down pedestrians? On the face of it, nothing, but insurance and credit analysts claim there's a very high correlation between folks with lousy credit and folks who file lots of claims. In the past few years, some state insurance commissions have tried to limit the practice of tying credit scores to insurance rates. In my home state of Michigan, however, the insurance lobbyists bought steak dinners for the tax-fattened hyenas in the state legislature and, miraculously, insurance companies can still use credit scores to set your rates. If you live in Massachusetts, Hawaii, or California, the practice is banned because, evidently, your state elects vegetarians.

The bad news is that making late payments inflicts real damage on your credit score, since your payment history makes up 35 percent of your score. The good news is that because timely payment is such a big factor in your credit score, you can boost it very easily just by paying on time. Make sure every bill gets paid before the due date for several months and you'll start to see your score improving. It won't help you immediately, but put a note in your calendar for six months or a year from now and go reprice your insurance to see if your credit score has improved enough by then to lower your rates.

Ask your insurance agent how your score stacks up. He or she is unlikely to give you the exact number but should be able to explain where you fall on the scale. You can buy the most widely used credit score from the folks at FICO at www.myFICO.com. You can get a free estimate of what your FICO score looks like by visiting Bankrate.com, the Web site I used to run.[2]

Not every company uses the same score, which is based on your credit history (there are several formulas out there), but if you look like a Boy Scout on one score, it's unlikely that another will decide you're less reliable than the average hobo.

Credit scores are a complex and sometimes murky world. Unlike your credit history, you can't get a free copy of your credit scores, and you can't dispute how they're constructed. Beyond paying all your bills on time there are other moves you can make to improve your score, from keeping old unused credit card accounts active to how much credit you use. The topic could fill a book and it has. For a complete guide to demystifying and raising your score, see the excellent *Your Credit Score, Your Money & What's at Stake* by Liz Weston.[3]

Pinching pennies so hard that Lincoln gets a headache

Cut your coverage to the bone and eliminate any extras on policies. Carry only the minimum coverage you need to stay legal and protected from a worse financial calamity if you get injured in an accident. If, for example, you have good medical, life, and disability insurance, make sure you don't duplicate that with more than the minimum required medical coverage for your auto policy.

One tactic that may seem drastic is moving. Depending on where you live, insurance companies may stick you with high rates or even refuse to write you a policy if they think the accident rate or auto theft is too high in your area. When I first moved to Florida in the 1980s, I called the company that had been insuring my car for three years, only to have the agent tell me that he wasn't allowed to issue coverage to single males under thirty in my zip code. It's probably not worth moving just to get lower insurance, but if you are relocating or coming up on the end of a lease, check out how your rates will be influenced by moving to another neighborhood.

Gas

Fuel is the most volatile transportation expense, since the price of gas fluctuates with every twitch of the economy or flare-up in Middle Eastern politics, which, because it's hot and there's sand everywhere, happens frequently. Gas, along with groceries, is also one of the items most strongly felt in your budget, since you fill up much more often than you buy a new water heater.

Freeing up cash

First, make sure you're getting the best price you can at the pump. Use an online service such as GasBuddy.com to find the lowest prices near your home or workplace and stick with the stations that consistently charge the least. This way you save every time you fill up without continually having to hunt around for a better deal.

If you have more than one car, use the one that gets the best mileage whenever you can, especially for long trips. There are few times it makes more sense to take my beloved Roadmaster wagon on a long trip instead of my wife's Honda, so, unless we're hauling the boat or the whole family and our luggage somewhere, we choose the thrifty five-speed manual Honda. You don't need to call up the FuelEconomy.gov Web site to calculate the mileage difference for a quick trip to the store, but for any long trip—especially one that you make regularly, such as my sixty-mile daily roundtrip drive to downtown Detroit—drive the car that gives you the best MPG.

It should go without saying that keeping your car well maintained makes a difference, and this includes paying close attention to your tire pressure. Try to check it once a week and consult the maintenance schedule in the owner's manual. Finally, take out the junk in the trunk. A sandbag back there may make sense to give you more traction in wintertime, but in summer you're just wasting gas. The same goes for those ten bags of newspapers you've been meaning to take to the recycling center for the last month.

Making ends meet

When possible, eliminate trips. Try carpooling or see if there are any mass transit options that make sense for your schedule and don't cost more than the gas you'd save by leaving the car at home. Check out monthly commuter passes for buses and trains, local ride-sharing services, commercial express buses, and van services, or see if your workplace offers carpooling opportunities.

If you are able to take advantage of mass transit, check to see if your employer offers a commuter benefit. Under IRS rules, you can pay for certain mass transit and even parking or bicycle commuting expenses with pretax dollars, which lowers your tax bill and increases your take-home pay. The benefit works like a flexible health care spending account. You can get more information at the IRS Web site[4] or from your benefits coordinator or human resources department at work.

Pinching pennies so hard that Lincoln gets a headache

You should consider parking the car and finding other ways to get around. For a two-car family, this could be a major inconvenience, but one that saves money. For a single person or a one-car family, it could be nearly impossible. But again, transportation is the second-biggest expense in most family budgets. If you can learn to live without a car, not only will you save on gas, insurance, and maintenance, but you can eliminate a car payment or even generate some cash from selling an unneeded car. By combining car pools, rides from friends, occasionally borrowing a car, or using a car-sharing service that offers short-term rentals, such as Zipcar, IGO, Relay-Rides, or through members of the CarSharing Association, it might be easier than you think to live without your car. And if you've got a car that sits unused for part of the week, you can offer your car for short-term rentals through such services, too.

One place you may not be able to save if you park your car and keep it is on insurance. Your insurance company may charge a hefty cancellation fee, up to a full year's premium in some cases. Also, your state department of motor vehicles will likely demand that you surrender your license plates once your insurance company reports that you've canceled your policy and no other insurer shows you taking a new one. If you can garage the car for several months and the insurance cancellation fee isn't too steep, completely taking your car off the road will cut a lot of spending out of your budget. For most of us, however, it may not be realistic. Chris Balish has lots of advice in his book *How to Live Well Without Owning a Car*, but it's not going to win him any friends here in Motown.[5]

The Bottom Line

Goal: $1,000

Week 1—Transportation . . . $41.61
Total monthly savings . . . $41.61

Left to cut . . . $958.39

I finally found some savings in our monthly gas costs. While I preferred to drive my prized Roadie daily and Mrs. Funny Money was loath to part with her Honda, the seven-mile-per-gallon difference hit us at the pump. The round trip to my office in the Buick cost more than $9 a day in gas, while the more fuel-efficient Honda burned $6.48 in gas. If I commuted in the Accord on the three days Mrs. Funny Money was at home, we used about thirteen gallons less in gas each month, producing savings of $35.30, based on EPA figures and a $2.70 average cost of regular gas.

That was in October 2009. Today that savings would be even better, since gas prices have steadily increased as the economy has picked up. By the end of 2012, the average price in the United States for a gallon of unleaded regular was $3.80, so we'd save almost $50 a month. On the other hand, Mrs. Funny Money has since upgraded from her Honda to a Mercury Mariner, which gets just two miles per gallon more than the Roadmaster. That works out to a meager savings of $15.83 per month, and demonstrates why managing your money is an ongoing chore.

Auto insurance didn't offer much savings either, since I already had a good deal. The one bright spot I could find was that switching from monthly billing to paying my premium every six months would save $54.87 on a six-month renewal. That cut $6.31 a month, for total auto savings of $41.61, leaving the first installment of my budget-cutting columns stuck in a $58.39 pothole.

$ 3

Miscellaneous

I Discover That All Kinds of Useless Spending
Indicates My Financial Common Sense
Also Is Locked in My Storage Unit

So, in the first installment of my "Grand Experiment" series, printed right there in the Monday issue of *The Detroit News* for all to see, I missed my $100 savings goal by $58.39 right out of the gate. This, I thought, must be what it felt like to be the guy behind New Coke.

All I could do was take comfort in the inspiring words of the great American inventor Thomas Alva Edison, who flopped time after time trying to invent the lightbulb. Said Edison: "I have not failed. I've just found ten thousand ways that won't work."

Admittedly, I'd only tried four ways to save, but I had nine more weeks to take the other 9,996 shots at it.

Looking for a quick success for my second column, my eye fell on the "miscellaneous" category of my budget, the metaphorical junk drawer of family finances. My real kitchen junk drawer is filled with useless stuff I haven't gotten around to throwing out—broken rubber bands, dried-up tubes of Krazy Glue, and a spare trunk key for my long-gone '76 Plymouth Volare.

The same goes for my financial junk drawer. It included an unused subscription to Weight Watchers Online, a forgotten e-mail account, an old life insurance policy, a subscription to an online baby-sitter directory, legal insurance, and a storage unit that hadn't been opened since about the time Geraldo ventured into Al Capone's vault.

What they all had in common was that they were automatically charged to my bank account or credit card. This made them easy to overlook each month and, I imagined, hard to eliminate. I'd have to plow through a bunch of papers, find contact numbers, and then call to cancel the services on top of deciding whether the family really needed any of this stuff. But there was the potential to save a lot of dough: there was a total of $181.42 in this category, so surely I could cancel enough stuff to hit my goal of cutting $100 for the second week of my series *and* make up some of the nearly $60 shortfall from the first week.

Your own "miscellaneous" category of recurring monthly bills is going to include lots of charges different from mine. Anything that you don't budget (assuming you have one) or pay as part of a larger set of expenses usually lands under the miscellaneous label. You can choose to recategorize things to their proper places, as I did with the old life insurance policy, or as I could have done by moving the baby-sitter subscription service to the child care portion of the budget. If you track your spending and categorize the transactions, just keep it consistent so you can easily figure out how much that subscription to *Cat Fancy* is costing you, even though Fluffy passed on to the Great Litter Box in the Sky two years ago.

No matter how you track an expense, your job right now is to decide whether you can cut it, and if you can't, whether you can find it for less. Don't get all tangled up obsessing about whether your auto insurance is part of your insurance category or your auto category. By the end of this whole process, you'll have the pretty good basics of a budget, having nailed down your top ten biggest monthly expenditures, and you should continue to refine it from there.

Right now, we're here to cut spending and free up cash, not create an elegantly color-coded, beautifully formatted spreadsheet that tracks every penny you spend with the ruthlessness of a Kardashian searching for a new husband.

Automated charges

If I had been getting a bill in the mail every month for an e-mail account I hadn't used in more than two years, then had to sit down, write out a check, dig out those nifty return-address labels that I just *know* are around somewhere, then look for a stamp, then go buy stamps, then remember where my wife keeps the stamps and realize I've wasted $12 buying stamps, I would not have been paying the bill for that old e-mail account for very long. So how did that account, which I was going to maintain for just a few months after we moved, live on, leeching my money for two years?

Easy. The charge, along with all the others, went on a credit card. Which was a great convenience when I needed the e-mail account. The bill got paid automatically, so there was no danger of the account being closed or of having late charges added, plus I had a convenient record for my taxes, and I gave the whole thing less thought than I devote to the World Indoor Soccer League. That kind of convenience works against you, however, when you no longer need what's behind that easy monthly charge.

Usually these kinds of charges spring from momentary good intentions that end up placing another brick in the road to debt hell. People want to lose weight, so they sign up for the ongoing gym membership at $29.95 a month. Or the healthy cooking Web site with a $9.95 monthly charge. After a few months, your self-improvement initiative loses steam, but canceling those charges seems like an admission of failure that would get piled on top of the guilt you already feel every thirty days when you see that charge on your credit card statement and realize you haven't hit the gym or whipped up those egg-white omelets for breakfast. Instead, you're back to sitting in front of the TV plowing through carry-out pizza, getting nearly as bloated as your credit card balance. The only thing getting thinner is your savings, as you cough up a couple hundred bucks a year in some kind of psycho-financial anorexic binge and purge.

Of course, that's assuming that you even stop and look through your monthly card statements. There are more than 600 million credit cards in circulation today, which works out to more than three for each U.S. household. Nearly one third of U.S. cardholders admitted to paying only the minimum balance at least once in the past year, according to the Federal Reserve Bank of Boston, and more than half were carrying a balance. I'm betting that plenty of us feel bad enough about our balances that we furtively open the envelope, look at the minimum payment due, and send out the check or online payment as quickly as possible to avoid dealing with the details of our debt.

But that's how a subscription here and a membership there pile up to weigh down your finances. And, as I sheepishly found, it's not all that tough to root them out. I hadn't touched my old e-mail account or the Weight Watchers subscription in years (wish I could say the same about nachos), but they were instantly canceled with just a few clicks on a Web site and a single phone call. What was really stupid is that I already got Weight Watchers help at work, complete with diet and food guides and recipes, which was why I never used the online service. My company's health plan paid for nearly all the cost of weekly Weight Watchers meetings conveniently located right in our office, including weigh-ins, or, as I called them, "Tuesdays with Shame."

The initial thrill of seeing that I had just saved close to $400 a year was wiped out by the realization that I had been an utter fool to let those expenses run unchecked for so long. But there's no sense in crying over spilled milk, especially when it's full-fat Grade A and you've known all along that you should be drinking skim.

The legal insurance was a keeper at $19.92 a month, especially since Mrs. Funny Money and I needed to update our wills. Plus, the coverage more than paid for itself when we hired attorneys to handle the purchase of Grandpa Verne's condo and the new place in Michigan.

One way to consider whether to keep or cancel this kind of recurring membership or service fee is to get away from the low, "E-Z monthly payment," which often doesn't *feel* like a lot of money, and look at your annual cost. Balance that against how often you use the plan or service, plus any expense you might incur in either canceling or restarting the membership if you need it later.

In this case, $19.92 per month adds up to $239 a year. Getting a simple will prepared would cost at least $250 for one person, and likely more in the case of me and Mrs. Funny Money, since our wills will be complicated by the need to provide for Li'l Money and the guardians lucky enough to get him (though they may feel differently if our untimely demise occurs during his teenage years). So, even if I carry the insurance for another two years, it should more than pay for itself, even if we don't experience any unforeseen legal hassles. Finally, the plan is a holdover from the benefits package at Mrs. Funny Money's old job and isn't offered at my workplace, meaning we'd have to sign up for a new, more costly one if we were to cancel it now and restart it in the future.

The same issues don't apply to the baby-sitting directory, since we have a roster of dependable, caring sitters for our boy and, if we cancel, we can simply resubscribe anytime down the road. So, Mrs. Funny Money agreed to add a couple of backup baby-sitters to our roster and then cancel the subscription. As for the e-mail account,

I'd kept it open after the move so that I could stay in touch with freelance clients and professional contacts. But, more than two years later, everyone had my new e-mail address and I never checked the account, which was stuffed with spam and notes from sexy Russians who had inherited fortunes from a Nigerian prince. It was canceled with a couple of phone calls and a few additional pangs of guilt about wasted cash.

Freeing up cash

No matter how much money you make or how comfortable your cash flow may be, there's no excuse to let forgotten recurring payments pile up. Like bank fees and late charges, it's understandable how this happens, but you're simply wasting money. If you don't go over your card statements in detail every month, start by reading through one statement this month, and cancel any unnecessary charges. If you only have one credit card, it'll be easy. If you're allowing some services to automatically debit charges to your checking account, do the same.

(I personally don't like to allow anyone to debit my checking account automatically, since it's much more difficult to dispute or reverse mistaken or inaccurate charges than it is with a credit card. If you don't qualify for a credit card or don't want the temptation of having one around, set up such payments as a recurring automated payment you make through your online checking account, where it's easier to monitor activity and cancel charges.)

When it comes to deciding whether to keep or cancel gym memberships and similar subscriptions, you can try to balance convenience, guilt, and good intentions against a few extra bucks per month, but that's not the best approach. Instead, try this: calculate the annual cost of your membership to, say, the discount buyers club at Shoe Lace Depot. (Their motto: "We'll help you tie one on!") At $12.95 a month, that's $155.40 a year plus, God forgive you, any interest charges that treacherously inflate the tab if you aren't paying off the new charges each month.

Now think about your biggest financial goal: at the end of the year, you can be more than 150 bucks closer to that goal, or you can fritter away the dough thinking you'll save a little money on designer shoe laces and shoe lace accessories. If your goal is paying down debt, you'll also save the interest charged on the $155.40 you can pay off in the next twelve months, and, if your goal is saving or investing, you'd get the interest or investment gains that money would generate.

Which would you rather have? As they say at Shoe Lace Depot, that decision's a tough one—knot!

Making ends meet

If your budget is really stretched, making decisions is easy: money beats convenience. Any subscription or service that you can get for free with online research, a trip to the library, or working with friends and neighbors needs to go. Take my Weight Watchers online bill: you can find Weight Watchers books and the monthly magazine at the library, or see if your company health plan offers a discount to attend the meetings (I promise I won't peek when you weigh in). As for the baby-sitter directory, you can find sitters by aggressively polling your friends, the parents of your kid's classmates, and Craigslist. Yes, it's a hassle to do the background checks on your own and track down each sitter's references, but your time is free (especially if your budget is tight because you're unemployed or have lost hours at work). I know many parents would be loath to give out the name and number of their favorite baby-sitters, but the next time you're cooking, make up an extra tray of lasagna and I'll give up the digits for Audrey. Just use ground turkey, not beef—weigh-in is tomorrow.

When it comes to canceling recurring charges that could cost more money to reinstate later, such as with my legal insurance, consider just how unknowable the future can be. A lot of things can happen between now and "someday" when I'll get around to updating my will, but if you really need to cut spending now, it's better to have cash in the hand today and solve any future needs later.

In fact, the more I consider that legal insurance, the closer it comes to violating my big $1,000 Challenge rule against spending money now to achieve some vague future savings. The best solution would be to get organized, get the will done now, and cancel the insurance. Then I get the best of both worlds: the necessary legal guidance *and* saving nearly $240 a year. So getting off my butt is a better strategy than spending and waiting. Especially in this case, where instead of a will I've had a won't.

That's not to say that more ambitious plans aren't worth keeping. As soon as my boy, Li'l Money, was born, his mother and I signed him up for Florida's prepaid college tuition plan for about $75 a month. That translates into a fully paid four-year college education at a discount of tens of thousands of dollars. That's one household expense we won't cancel for anything short of a zombie invasion.

If you can't make that kind of strong, bottom-line argument for small conveniences and mental indulgences, like an abandoned diet plan or health club membership, then it needs to go. If you feel hassled driving to the community center to work out instead of going to your fancy gym, just think about the money you're saving.

I understand that many people will balk at sacrificing their physical fitness routine for fiscal fitness. While it's not hard to maintain a healthy weight, it's just so much easier to pack on extra pounds. That's particularly true during the holidays, such as Arbor Day, Canadian Thanksgiving, and International Day of Peace. (Especially if, like me, you observe International Day of Peace at the International House of Pancakes.)

In my case, I skip the pricey big-name gym for a local workout studio run by a chipper young woman whose idea of fun is a five-mile sprint. Kerry's group training classes are less expensive than a session with a personal trainer or a monthly gym membership, and she gives me a discount for buying ten classes at a time. The prepaid classes don't expire, so if I miss a session, I'm not out any money.

But that doesn't mean I don't pay in other ways. Kerry recently had me sit on a huge rubber ball and commence a series of sit-ups. This was to work my abs. Or maybe my bicuspids. I huffed, puffed, and ooffed, trying to work around my swollen gut.

"I know just how you feel," Kerry sympathized, before adding just the encouragement a middle-aged man is surely paying a personal trainer to provide. "I had the same problem when I was pregnant with my daughter."

Pinching pennies so hard that Lincoln gets a headache

Unless it's an essential service that you absolutely need now, and you can't replace it or live without it, cut it. Check the library, see if you can pool a purchase with friends (say, for example, splitting the cost of the sitter service subscription with other families that just had babies), or find a way to live without it. Another example: instead of holding on to my old e-mail account for years, I could have kept it for one month, sent out a weekly e-mail blast to everyone in the address book giving them my new e-mail address, and then canceled it. Other than sheer laziness, I can't recall why I didn't do that in the first place.

The sad truth is that if you're really up against the wall when it comes to money, you're going to have to learn to do without a lot of luxuries and everyday conveniences. Once you've finished going through the big categories of your spending as you work through this book, keep going through every dollar of recurring expenses. In my case, a little here and a little there added up to $1,000 of savings per month. I was, quite frankly, embarrassed at how sloppy and wasteful I'd been, although, as any physics major will tell you, it takes effort to overcome inertia, whether physical or financial. For a whole host of reasons, it's easier to avoid digging through your finances, but it pays off, especially when you're in trouble.

When times are really tough, consider the advice of Mary Hunt, founder of DebtProofLiving.com: "If it isn't necessary for the preservation of life or to keep Mommy and Daddy out of jail, don't spend it."

Storage unit

It's often said that you can't put a price on memories, but I do it every month: $76.

That's the tab for a storage unit packed with childhood books, stuffed animals, and at least one old baseball glove. It was the biggest charge every month in our miscellaneous spending category. At least I wasn't alone: according to the Self Storage Association, in 2011 10.8 million households spent $22.45 billion (yes, with a "B") to store our stuff.

It's not about the stuff, but what that stuff represents, whether it's Grandma's china or the trophy for "Most Improved Camper 1969." We don't want Grandma's china—we want Grandma. I have a much nicer fishing rod than the old fiberglass one in storage that my late father gave me. And even if I did use the old one, it would never reel in what I really want—my dad.

Hanging onto those memories comes at a cost: more than $900

a year for me. That's the price of a nice weekend getaway with Mrs. Funny Money, summer day camp for Li'l Money, or a solid contribution to our retirement account. Instead, I've got old, useless stuff and bills to store it.

What I needed to do was take a lesson from my friend Judy Kelner, who decided to pull her late grandma's good china out of the attic and put it to everyday use. When one of her grandkids drops a plate, Judy lifts her eyes and briefly prays, "Thank you, Grandma." Then she gets out the dustpan and pitches the broken pieces.

So, it was time to cancel one more recurring monthly charge and take my boy to clean out that storage unit together. There's an old baseball glove that's been waiting for him a long time.

Freeing up cash

If you've got a lot of stuff, you can take the time to sort out the unit, sell off anything that can fetch a decent price, clear out space at home, and donate or trash the rest. If you're a pack rat like me, ask yourself this question before you keep anything: This thing has been locked in storage for X years and I've managed to live without it. Do I really need a spare Veg-O-Matic? Even if it's the baby blanket Great-grandma knitted for you, you're better off taking a nice picture for your scrapbook, then sending it to your cousin's pregnant daughter and making sure it continues to circulate among your family rather than allow it to gather dust. And it's cheaper.

Making ends meet

Time is money, and the more time you keep that junk in storage, the less money you are going to have. Get over your inertia by gathering family or friends and setting aside an afternoon to empty that locker. Set it up like a moving party. You can distribute things you don't want among your helpers, haul the rest back to your place, and then buy a couple of pizzas and bottles of cheap red wine for a celebration of your newfound fiscal responsibility. Going through your personal belongings may unearth a few unflattering details about your life, so make sure these are your real friends, the kind of friends who will, for example, pledge to forget that you were paying good money to stash the entire collected works of Captain & Tennille.

Pinching pennies so hard that Lincoln gets a headache

Haul it all out ASAP. Then try to squeeze every dime out of your detritus by selling your stuff on Craigslist, the consignment store, or eBay (or through an eBay consignment shop). Anything you can't sell you donate, making sure to snap some pictures and write down detailed descriptions so that you can take a tax write-off later. You can estimate the value of your donations at SalvationArmyUSA .org.[1] Even though you may not have much income to be taxed, more write-offs will lower your taxable income and can help you qualify for refundable tax credits that will prompt the Treasury to send you a check at tax time.

Because you're financially stressed and it seems like a big hassle to deal with all this stuff—along with any emotions attached to belongings left behind by a divorced spouse or deceased loved one— you may be tempted to stop paying the storage bill and just forfeit your goods. Hey, maybe your junk will end up starring on an episode of *Storage Wars*, right?

While it's true that the laws in all states allow storage companies to auction your stuff if you've abandoned it, the storage company can come after you for any unpaid rental balance—along with late fees and penalties. You've got enough problems, so don't add to them by having your credit dinged and a collection agency hounding you. Better to gather your friends (one of whom, ideally, has a pickup), schlep the stuff, and get it over with. If you can't swing the pizzas, turn it into a potluck. Good friends will not only understand, but they'll want to help. Although, when you all get back to your apartment, they are going to insist that you refrain from playing "Muskrat Love." Let's face it: friendship goes only so far.

Life insurance, part I

Although the storage unit clearly needed to go, whether to cancel or keep my old life insurance policy wasn't so obvious, so I turned to a few experts. This is going to be just a brief foray into the wonderful world of insurance and risk management, with a more extensive discussion of life insurance, disability insurance, and more coming in chapter 9, so try not to die or get yourself dismembered before then.

Cutting life insurance coverage is a risky play, said Peter Bahner, a certified life underwriter who also heads the Great Lakes–area practice for Prudential Financial. Bahner told me that he's seen clients cancel a policy for a year or two, then run into a health issue that makes it very costly—or impossible—to get coverage later. Even reducing coverage on a policy, which can lower the premiums, may require a new medical review that could turn up issues that would raise your premium instead of lowering it.

"You never want to cancel a policy until you have replacement coverage in place," Bahner warned. "I don't think that risk is worth the savings."

On the other hand, the $100,000 policy is a small part of my life insurance and would produce only $5,000 or $6,000 of income a year for my grieving family. In this instance, Bahner said, it might not hurt to cancel it. But on the *other* other hand (like economists, personal finance experts usually need at least three hands to make any decision), $28 a month for $100,000 in coverage is a pretty good buy according to Fran Twiddy, a certified financial planner who runs Independent Financial Advisors of Redford. "That's a cheap policy," she told me. "I would hate to give that up."

Twiddy added that as we get older, insurability can be an issue. If I really want to save, she said, I should take a page from my auto insurance playbook and go from monthly to annual payments, which could cut from 4 percent to 8 percent of my annual cost.

Calculating all our insurance needs showed that the $100,000 policy was necessary to reach the total annual income I'd need to leave behind for the Widow Funny Money. (Arriving at that number is an entirely different equation we'll discuss in chapter 9, when I tackle our overall insurance bill.) So that monthly expense was a keeper.

The Bottom Line

Goal: $1,000

Week 1—Transportation . . . $41.61
Week 2—Miscellaneous . . . $132.89
Total monthly savings . . . $174.50

Left to cut . . . $825.50

So, the insurance stayed. The grand total: $132.89 of spending eliminated by canceling an old e-mail account, Weight Watchers online, a subscription to an online baby-sitting directory, and the storage unit. That hit the $100 goal for Week 2 and pushed the total savings to $174.50 a month, knocking down the first week's savings shortfall to a mere $25.50.

This meant it was time to celebrate. I decided to splurge and open a good bottle of wine. Or at least I would have. I'd swear that corkscrew was somewhere in the junk drawer.

4

Utilities

Your Author Plugs into Savings, Rings up
Lower Bills, and Cackles Maniacally While
Visiting Revenge upon His Cable Company

Now that I had hit my $100 weekly savings goal for the first time, I was tantalizingly close to breaking even in Week 3. My goal was to not only come up with another hundred bucks, but also to find a few more to cut so I could make up the rest of the Week 1 shortfall.

Fortunately, the prospects for savings looked good because the category for Week 3 was utilities, including water, cable TV, phone, and more. If it came out of a wall at my house, it was fair game for a cut. And thanks to new technology, online scams, and my own previously established sloth, it looked like I'd more than achieve my goal.

I took particular glee at wielding the budget ax in this case because, like every good American, it's my twenty-first-century right to absolutely hate my cable company. Between the $100-plus bill every month and the service with a scowl, I found despising the cable guys nearly as easy as hating professional soccer and light beer.

The other night, for example, Mrs. Funny Money was working. I was tired and just wanted a little mindless entertainment before bed, so I scrolled through our two-hundred-channel lineup of cable offerings. Jeez, I said "mindless," not "mind-numbing"! The first dozen shows were reality fare so dim-witted that I could feel the idiocy seeping into my DNA, to the point where I was putting my great-grandchildren at the risk of being born stupid. The next twenty channels were pay-per-view events, such as the New Guinea Little League Junior Putt-Putt semifinals ($24.95). That was followed by a bunch of shopping channels, at which point I gave up and read a book because it turns out that *Tips for the Perfect-Fitting Bra* was nothing like what I'd imagined.

This shoddy menu of entertainment had me more steamed than a bowl of clams when I considered our cable bill. My first call was to an alternate cable provider that operates in our county. Unfortunately, they didn't serve our neighborhood. A few more calls to compare service got me a package from my phone and Internet provider, AT&T. Thanks to the widespread use of fiber-optic cable I found a combined package that kept all of my current lineup while also dumping a movie channel I never watched, but which the old cable company required me to take to get the movie channel I do watch. That cut a combined bill of $225.84 for cable, phone, and Internet access to $145, for a savings of $80.84. The U-verse package included unlimited long distance, too, so I could cancel our long-distance carrier, which averaged $3.60 a month.

I briefly considered inviting our cable provider to make a counteroffer, but the lousy customer service, frequent lineup changes and service outages, and craptastic tech support gave me no reason to want to continue doing business with that bunch of dunces. Plus, any savings they could offer would be nowhere as valuable as the glee I experienced in calling to cancel. I felt like Rhett Butler storming out of Tara in *Gone with the Wind*, but instead of growling, "Frankly, my dear, I don't give a damn," I was cackling like the Joker in *The Dark Knight*. Also, the mansion is in flames.

But wait—as they say on late-night TV ads—there was more! My old, slow Internet service had been with AT&T, at a cost of $44.95 a month when I'd signed up four years ago, but that price had dropped. All I had to do at any point was call to get the lower rate, the service rep told me, but I had never asked. The rep refunded two months of the overpayments. In addition, my new TV-phone-Internet services came with introductory prices that saved a combined $324 during the first six months. I also got a $200 AT&T gift card.

To cap it off, a bogus "third-party" voice mail service had somehow become added to my phone account. Buried in the list of charges was $14.95 every month for something called Orbit Telecom voice mail, some kind of Web-based voice messaging service. Someone in the house—likely my son, Li'l Money—clicked on a pop-up ad while browsing the Web and unwittingly signed us up. That was easily canceled with a call to Orbit, while the AT&T service rep refunded the charges.

Phone, cable, and Internet

These three services are increasingly interconnected, and saving on one often depends on increasing your use of another. The easiest option is to look at bundles of services, which can include cell phone service, too. For maximum savings, you should consider unbundling, but that's going to take more time and research. The trade-off of convenience versus money is a common one, and you don't know if it's going to be worth the extra trouble until after you've identified your potential savings. Still, it's worth a try if you can spare a little time.

Freeing up cash

Each regular monthly bill in the house—especially utilities—should get a thorough going-over every year or two if you want to keep a lid on costs. Plans for cable TV packages or cell phone service are ever-changing, introductory deals expire, and service charges mysteriously appear, while new competitors show up to offer more attractive deals. A thorough audit of each charge on a bill and an hour or two of comparison shopping can be more than worth your while.

Even if you don't move any part of your service, start with the easy stuff, which, I have to add once again, carries the risk of making you feel really, really dumb. Comb your statement for the kinds of add-on charges like the Web messaging service I discovered. Not only did I not order the service, but since I didn't know it was there, I had never even used it. I simply overlooked it on my bill, month after month. Over the course of six months, that was nearly $90 down the drain.

It doesn't have to be some borderline scam, either, but might be charges for services that you once thought sounded good but you no longer use. A second phone number, a long-distance plan, a bunch of features like three-way calling or call forwarding. any of these may have outlived their usefulness and can be trimmed from your bill with no inconvenience at all.

Even if you don't feel like comparison shopping, simply call your phone company (if you're a fossil like me who insists on maintaining a landline), cable provider, or whatever and ask for a cheaper plan or any new discounts. That's what happened with my Internet access—the price just dropped over time. Or your cable company may have introduced a new package that allows you to get your favorite channels at a lower price. The phrase "Money for the asking" directly applies here. So does "Dialing for dollars." So does "Are you nuts? Pick up the phone and stop wasting your money!"

Making ends meet

You should definitely be bargain hunting on all this stuff: cable, Internet, phone, and long-distance plans. But you also should be looking at eliminating these services where you can. Let's start with your phone line.

If you have Internet access at home, you can skip your local phone company and use a service that routes your calls over the Internet using the Voice over Internet Protocol (VoIP). You can keep your number (usually for a fee), and you'll have to buy some kind of box to attach to your net connection. Monthly fees are anywhere from $5 to $30, and setup fees are about $30. You may also have to pay some local taxes and access fees, but you already pay those with your regular landline. There also may be cancellation fees, so make sure you get thirty days or more to try the service before you're locked in. Skype, magicJack, Net2Phone, Vonage, and Ooma are just a few of the providers. One feature to look for with these virtual phone services is Enhanced 911, where the provider assigns an address to your number so that fire, police, and other emergency responders can locate you if you make an emergency 911 call.

This assumes you have home Internet access—but do you need it? If you use a smartphone or tablet with wireless connectivity and don't do a lot of heavy online work, your cellular connection may give you all the Web access you need to simply check e-mail, post Facebook updates, and handle other online tasks with apps or a mobile browser. (I don't even consider perusing Craigslist and eBay because that's why we go to work, right?) You also can try using your smartphone as a mobile hotspot and connecting your computers to the Internet that way, especially if you have one of those increasingly hard-to-find unlimited data plans. Then you can cancel your home Internet. But that means you either need to keep a conventional landline if you want a home phone, or cut the cord completely and depend solely on your cell phone.

The point is to avoid paying for the same thing twice. When money is tight, having two ways of making phone calls or two ways of accessing the Internet means you've got at least one way to save. So weigh the options and add up the costs. The deciding factor is what's going to keep your total utility costs lowest. If accessing the Web through your smartphone means you'll be piling up big mobile data charges, then keeping home Internet access makes sense, and stick with a simple, dumb-style cell phone. You're going to have to check the options, get prices, then get out a sheet of paper and add it all up to find the least expensive way of meeting your needs.

The cheapest calling option might be to keep a basic landline and ditch your cell phone altogether. If you're the kind of person who actually enjoys having periods of time when you can't be reached by your boss, relatives, or automated calls with credit card offers from "Rachel," you may find this option not only frugal but downright appealing. But I do realize that today, asking people to go without a cell phone is like asking them to live without eyebrows.

When it comes to cable service, I think we pretty much need to establish that this is a luxury, although it's one that varies according to your lifestyle and location. I've lived in New York City for two different stretches without a TV and I was happy not to have one. The first time, after college, I was just too flat broke to buy one. Then, by the time I did have the scratch to buy a TV, I'd found so many fascinating people and places in the city that I didn't have time to watch it. The second time I was a graduate fellow and realized that even reruns of *Gilligan's Island* would be more interesting than grinding through macroeconomics, so, in one of the few wise decisions I can say I've ever made, I focused on my studies and once again went TV-less.

It's not that I'm one of those anti-TV snobs, and even if I were, having a youngster will pretty much beat that right out of you when you witness the calming powers *Bear in the Big Blue House* has over a distressed toddler. Still, we need to agree that any family could live just fine without expensive cable service. Consider canceling all but basic cable and augmenting your viewing with a Netflix subscription and videos from your local library. If you've got a high-definition (HD) television (or add a set-top converter for an older TV set) you can get high-definition broadcast signals with just the addition of an appropriate HD antenna. The Consumer Electronics Association has even created a Web site designed to help you figure out which type of antenna you need.[1] TiVo, the folks behind the digital video recording service, makes a TiVo box that accesses and records HD programming, too. Just combining HD broadcast and rentals from Netflix, the Redbox at your supermarket, or borrowing from the library gives you a good range of entertainment choices right there. You've got *Modern Family* and *The Hunger Games*, but you'll have to learn to live without *Game of Thrones* until you can pick up the DVD of the last season at your library.

When it comes to accessing cable channels without cable service, there are more and more online options every day, and they all leave me more and more confused. Using one of these will require you to keep Internet access, possibly at a higher speed than you're paying for now. There are streaming options over the Web, such as Hulu, and there all manner of little black boxes that will connect the Web to your television and give you access to most—but not all—programming for a monthly subscription charge. TiVo Premiere service offers most cable channels, and there are gizmos available from Apple TV, Roku, Vizio, Simple.TV, and probably two new ones that went into business as I typed that last sentence. You also have options through Amazon and iTunes and even through game systems such as Xbox and Wii.

Since I am one of the olds, I asked a smart young whippersnapper at work about all of it. Kevin uses some combination of three of these things, and, from what I could gather, saves money and is very happy with all of it. That was all I could gather, though, because after he said, "Yeah, it works pretty good . . . ," I had no earthly idea what he was talking about. Still, I gleaned enough information to figure this out: be careful.

If you start signing up for new streaming TV subscriptions or buy a set-top box, HDMI cables, or even a new HDTV set, you are going to defeat the whole budget-cutting goal. You also may not want to invest the time or undergo what is guaranteed to be some level of tech frustration to get everything working together. But, if you have the time and the inclination (or access to the kind of handy twelve-year-old geek who amuses himself by wiring toaster ovens to activate the Death Star), you can try it. But let's make this ground rule: any outlay of cash that you "invest" in an effort to reduce your cable bill must pay for itself within six months or less. Yes, I am giving you a temporary dispensation from one of The $1,000 Challenge commandments ("Thou shalt not spend to save"), so don't abuse it.

Try this approach: First, create a list of programs and channels you regularly watch. Next, figure out if any of your existing technology can give you access to all, most, or some of it. Now research the simplest, least expensive options to fill in the gaps (*not* the coolest, latest, all-in-one gizmo that will impress your friends and allow you to remotely monitor the tire pressure on your backyard gas grill). Add it all up, and if it results in a lower ongoing monthly cost than cable *and* the savings covers any "capital outlay" (I love to sling that biz-school lingo!) of cash in six months or less, go ahead and try it. If not, cut down to basic cable or survive on broadcast TV and hit the DVD shelves at the library.

Pinching pennies so hard that Lincoln gets a headache

If you use a cell phone, kill the landline or vice versa (we'll talk about saving on cell phone plans in a bit). You're going to have to live with one phone. You'll also need to cancel cable and Internet. Yes, it's harsh, but we're desperate here. You can get movies and DVDs of TV shows at the library or learn to live with broadcast TV using the HDTV tactics described earlier. Hit pawnshops and consignment stores for videos for yourself and the kids. (A warning: You may be thrilled to find *Old Yeller* for 99 cents, but you're going to use up twice that much in tissues when Travis gets out his rifle toward the end. And you'll definitely need to keep the family dog out of the room, unless you need to send a message about what happens to mutts that chew on the dining room furniture.)

Young ones are especially unlikely to miss cable if you substitute a selection of videos to play over and over and over and over. And over. Even when we had all kinds of costly premium cable at the house, Li'l Money insisted on watching the same Disney *Sing Along Songs* video so many times that as long as I live—and no matter how hard I try—I will never, ever forget every note of Billy Joel singing "Why Should I Worry" from *Oliver & Company*. (He's got "street savoir faire," which—I think we all can agree—in a just world would be a painfully debilitating venereal disease.) My only defense was to get the kid hooked on *The Jungle Book* because you never do get tired of Louis Prima swinging away on "I Wan'na Be Like You." (Added benefit: you get the housework done a *lot* faster.)

I think the only time you should consider keeping home Internet access when times are tough is if you are freelancing or working from home and need access to keep that money coming in. I know the Web is essential to any job search, but you don't need 24/7 access, so use the library. (In fact, it's probably healthier for you and better for your job hunt if you don't sit there in your underwear, nursing a Piels

Light while endlessly hitting "refresh" on SimplyHired.com at 2 in the morning.) If you've got a trusting neighbor and you both are stringent with your browser security, considering splitting the cost of access with someone else nearby and sharing a Wi-Fi connection. Avoid coffee shops with free Wi-Fi if you're going to feel guilty and end up paying $12 for a cappuccino to "rent" your table at Meanie Beanie's House of Likeable Lattes. Remember: cheap is good, but free is better.

I know that giving up the little things feels like a big thing when you're strapped. I know you're used to coming home and flipping on *The Real Housewives of Ishpeming* and checking in on Facebook or Foursquare. You feel like, "How can I be so broke that I can't afford this?" But those little things add up to big expenses, and you need to strip things down to the bare bones.

All I can suggest is to be proud of what you accomplish in shaving your expenses down to keep yourself afloat until things improve. Knowing that, whatever happens, you can get by for now can be very empowering, and, when your financial crisis passes, it will be a great source of strength. If you did get that 99-cent *Old Yeller* DVD, you'll recall that at one point, the father counsels, "Now and then, for no good reason, life will haul off and knock a man flat."

Yes, it does. Just do what you need to do to get back up.

Cell phones

When it came to cell phone service, I wasn't all that eager to shop around. In Metro Detroit, Verizon Wireless is consistently rated as having the best coverage, and, since I mostly use my cell phone as a phone, not a music player or gaming device, that's the most important consideration, especially since I'm a reporter *and* I drive an eighteen-year-old car. But that didn't mean I couldn't find savings here, too.

As soon as I called to ask about lowering my bill, I instantly knocked off $10 a month thanks to a new service plan. I was able to save another $15 because a cheaper data plan had been introduced. Finally, I saved $15 more by canceling a broadband connection option I "temporarily" added before vacation so that I could use my cell phone as a modem for my laptop. Then, of course, I forgot to cancel it, and the charge wound up on every bill for months afterward. All told, it was another $40 of savings in one short phone call.

Freeing up cash

The best bet is to compare service and coverage and comparison shop, if there's a good alternative provider. This is a lot easier now that consumers have the right to keep the same cell phone number, unlike the olden days, when we put up with unbelievable tons of crap from cell phone carriers because we were desperate to hang on to the phone number that was the only point of contact for friends, family, freelance clients, and old girlfriends who drunk-dial you at 3 a.m.

Once again, look over the bill for add-ons, like my broadband connection option, or some mobile messaging service, ring-tone subscription, or other nonsense you may have accidentally added or that may have been crammed on by a scammer. Finally, ask if you're eligible for any discounts based on where you work, go to school, or some other affiliation. For example, I get an 8 percent discount on my cell service because I'm a AAA member.

Start with reviewing how many minutes of calls, how many texts, and much data you're using every month. Typically, when you sign up for a cell phone plan, you're guessing at how much time you'll use each month. Then, once you've got a plan, you tend to stick with it, even if you're wildly overpaying for time you don't use.

If you've underestimated, you know it right away because you get hit with overage charges and you select a new plan, but if you overestimated your usage, the tendency is to just keep overpaying with a sense of relief that you aren't racking up extra charges.

Because we didn't grow up with cell phones, Mrs. Funny Money and I didn't start out as big texters. Asking someone over forty to send a text message is like asking him to run a marathon on his thumbs. It's easier—and usually faster—for us to simply drive over and talk to you. Of course, since it's a cell *phone*, we dimwitted olds often try to call people or even leave voice messages. Youngsters frown on phones being used for voice transmission, however, and look at someone my age making a call on an iPhone as if we were using it to chisel messages onto a cave wall.

As our friend's children became old enough to have phones (which is what, twenty-eight months now?), their parents bit the bullet and learned how to text their kids, then turned their newfound thumb savvy on us, their friends who've known them since the days when we all bought eight-tracks together. Then our babysitters were increasingly only available via text. Then they hired those snotty kids at work who text you from the next desk, asking you to please move your walker off their iPad charging cord. So, Mrs. Funny Money and I were dragged into the texting universe, although, since both of us are writers and editors, our messages employ fully spelled-out words *and* punctuation. Yes, when I use a semicolon in a text message it is with a conjunctive verb to connect related thoughts, *not* because I am winking at you.

Because we were infrequent texters, our original cell plans didn't include any text messaging coverage at all; it was cheaper to pay for each message. But as the messages picked up and coworkers started texting "LOL" to us during meetings, the charges mounted. (And why do you do that? I am in the same meeting. I can see and hear you laughing, so I don't need to know that it's "out loud," do I?) The real culprit behind our ever-rising text message bills was, of course, Li'l Money, who continued to do amazingly cute things that my wife would photograph with her cell phone camera to instantly share so that I could be reminded at any moment that both his childhood and my life were slipping away. That will be another 50 cents, sir. And this time, please don't pay in Indian-head pennies.

During a recent month, our text messages totaled more than $20, so it was time to shop for another plan for the Funny Money family and another reminder that change is a constant, especially when it comes to finances. Left ignored, those text charges will hurt, and, as the kids text, "IAGTKOM" (I Ain't Got That Kind of Money). LOL, or, as we grown-ups used to say, "Ha!"

Making ends meet

If you drop your landline and make your cell phone your one and only point of contact, keep an eye on your bill. Your voice usage may go up, resulting in higher charges that shrink—or entirely eat up— any savings. Monitor your usage and adjust your calling plan to keep the costs manageable.

If you're not locked into a contract, do some aggressive comparison shopping. One good comparison site is BillShrink.com, which can log on to your wireless account, analyze your calling patterns, and recommend alternatives. (I didn't find it to be entirely accurate in estimating my current monthly costs, however, so double-check the calculations against a few of your recent bills. The recommended plans did, however, save me about $40 a month.) Also check out prepaid cell phone plans, especially ones that will let you roll over any unused minutes from month to month, which can make sense if you aren't a heavy caller.

If you are locked into a contract, you may face a big early termination fee if you try to switch carriers. Talk to your service provider and get the best deal you can while you wait for your contract to expire, or balance your monthly savings against the termination fee and see if you'll come out ahead soon enough to make paying the fee worthwhile. Before you give up and stick with a plan, though, do a little homework on the Web to see if you are entitled to quit without a penalty. If, for example, your contract terms changed, that may allow you to exit your contract without penalty. Another option is to see if cutting down to the cheapest possible calling plan for the rest of your contract is cheaper than the termination fee. If so, make that move, cancel the contract when it expires, and sell your old phone to get back some of the dough.

Pinching pennies so hard that Lincoln gets a headache

If ditching a landline for a cell phone is your cheapest option, use all the tactics described above. And one more: if you have family members or a close friend with one of those all-inclusive family plans, ask if you can join the plan and contribute a few bucks a month toward their costs.

Another option is the Lifeline program. Under a program sponsored by the Federal Communications Commission, if your income is 135 percent of the poverty level (about $20,000 for a family of two) or less, you qualify for one discount prepaid wireless phone per household. You also qualify if you receive certain types of aid, such as Head Start for your child, Temporary Assistance for Needy Families, or Medicaid. This service is provided by the federal Universal Service Fund, which you've paid for years as part of your phone bill, so don't be shy about claiming the benefit if you now qualify. You can check your eligibility and find Lifeline providers in your state by going to lifelinesupport.org[2], or call the Universal Service Administrative Company (which administrates the program) at 888-641-8722, the FCC at 888-CALL-FCC, or your local telephone company. And hey, those toll-free numbers cost you when you dial from a cell phone, so find a landline to make those "free" calls.

Water, gas, and electricity

Tackling the big utility expenses such as water, gas, and electricity was just too involved for a one-week cost-cutting experiment, so I largely skipped these costs. Usually, saving here involves complicated, long-term options that require shelling out serious cash, such as drilling a well, installing energy-efficient windows and insulation, or buying a solar water heater. These tactics may pay off over several years, but I was looking to save *now*, and I wasn't going to pay out big bucks today to save a few dollars a month some day after the Detroit Lions win Super Bowl CCCXCVII (that's 397 to us non-Romans).

Yes, I know the federal government offers tax credits of up to 30 percent of the cost for making certain energy-efficient improvements to your home. But that means you still pay the other 70 percent. It's a great investment, but until you've got other financial priorities taken care of and can save to pay for those improvements up front, leave them for another day.

In the meantime, you should certainly take all the steps you can to conserve water, electricity, and gas. You can start with a home energy audit from your electric company. While the inspector might recommend some expensive improvements, chances are there'll be some small ones, too. So change those lightbulbs, turn off your computer at night, and clean your refrigerator coils.

A programmable thermostat can be a good addition that's not

too expensive, but the savings often aren't as big as you might expect. One study in Florida found home-cooling costs went up when adjustable thermostats were installed because residents set the temperature lower for the times when they were home. It mostly depends on your consistency in programming the thing and the temperatures you select—just the same as with a manual thermostat. Either way, saving on heating and cooling costs means more blankets and sweaters in the winter and more T-shirts, shorts, and fans in the summer.

If you've got an air conditioner, see whether your electric utility offers a plan that puts your AC on a separate electrical meter and gives the utility the option to briefly turn it off during periods of peak electricity use. The CoolCurrents plan, which won't turn off your AC for more than fifteen minutes every half hour, limited to eight hours during a 24-hour period, gives Metro Detroit homeowners discounted rates on electricity for their air-conditioning. DTE Energy estimates that homeowners can save up to 20 percent off their air-conditioning costs this way.

Naturally, you should fix leaky faucets and drop a bottle of water in the toilet tank to reduce the cost of each flush (avoid the old brick technique, since it can dissolve and send sediment into your plumbing). To cut down on watering lawns and gardens, look for free mulch and try your hand at some xeriscaping to keep things from getting brown. Local power companies trim a lot of trees that grow to interfere with power lines. They'll often run the branches and other wood through a chipper and offer the somewhat rough mulch free for the taking.

Level billing is a utility option that doesn't really save you money but does make it easier to pay your bills and plan your budget. It takes your annual gas, electric, or water bill and divides it up evenly for the next twelve months so that you have one consistent payment instead of a $60 gas bill in July and a $250 one in January. At the end of your twelve months, the bill adjusts to reflect current prices and your actual usage. Not every utility company offers these plans, but if yours does, it adds a welcome bit of predictability to your monthly cash flow.

Saving on all the major utilities comes down to common sense and conservation: the less you use, the less you pay. Shut the heat registers in empty rooms, use the toaster oven instead of the big oven, defrost the freezer, etc. Use all the resource-reducing tactics you can find. Plus, while you're saving money, you can help save the planet. This is important because, if the planet gets so polluted that we have to escape to Newt Gingrich's fifty-first state moon colony, you can just imagine what HBO is gonna charge to get *Curb Your Enthusiasm* at the Sea of Tranquility.

The Bottom Line

Goal: $1,000

Week 1—Transportation . . . $41.61
Week 2—Miscellaneous . . . $132.89
Week 3—Utilities . . . $139.39
Total monthly savings . . . $313.89

Left to cut . . . $686.11

I made the week's $100 goal plus covered all the shortfall from Week 1 and a few extra bucks to boot. That left me with $686.11 still to cut. Adding it all up, my immediate savings from a few phone calls came to $139.39 in ongoing monthly savings, plus $653.80 (!) in temporary discounts or refunds, including the $200 gift card.

Besides the savings, I finally got to walk over to the cable box and do something I've been itching to do for years—flip off my cable company.

5

Kid Costs

We Discover How a 99-Cent Margarita
Deployed at Just the Right Moment Turns
into a Lifetime Tab of $286,860

The next target on my list was the "Kid Costs" category. That meant focusing on expenses related to my boy, Funny Money Jr., or, as we call him, Li'l Money ('cuz that's all he leaves us). This was a tough one. His food and other costs were in with the rest of the family budget. And, since he was seven years old at the time, he didn't run up extra bills, such as sports leagues, car insurance, or bail.

All the other kid categories offered little hope of savings, from his bargain-priced college savings plan to nominal public school fees. My wife finds incredible bargains on his clothes, and I occasionally root through the office supply cabinet for school supplies. (You run a few grease pencils under a hacksaw and tell me that isn't the same thing as crayons.) Knocking out his summer day camp seemed like an option, but I realized any savings there would be more than offset by his mother's increased spending on prescriptions and tequila.

The bean counters at the U.S. Department of Agriculture regularly take some time off from counting beans to tote up the costs of raising a child. The most recent price tag: $286,860 to get a kid to age eighteen when adjusted for inflation from 2010 onward. And that doesn't even include some crucial expenses of the teenage years, such as iPods, car fenders, and tattoo removal.

This puts kids near the top of the list of luxury goods these days in the United States, if you define luxury goods as "something hardly anyone can afford." That's the case for lots of recession-racked families in the United States. As of 2009, according to the National Center for Health Statistics, the U.S. birthrate dropped from the record high of 4.3 million babies in 2007 to 4.1 million—the lowest in a century.

The perfect time to figure how you'll pay for a kid is before you have one running around, soaking up juice boxes and your every last dime. One advantage the Funny Money family had was the fact that we had our son after most of our friends spawned, and they were only too happy to deluge us with their unused baby materiel, from cribs to play castles to Barney tapes (I never will forgive you for the big purple demon, Rory!). So much baby stuff was dumped on us that the house took on the look of a Lilliputian landfill. We never visited the home of anyone with children when we didn't leave with bags of bottles, squeaky toys, and footed onesies. Our friends, Gretchen and Steve, once completely disassembled a five-foot-high plastic playhouse and stuffed the entire thing into the back of my Roadmaster wagon while I was getting a second helping of potato salad on their patio.

More than once, as we left a friend's house toting armloads of baby paraphernalia, the front door closed on the beginnings of a marital squabble that went almost exactly like this:

Husband: Why'd you give them all the baby clothes? What if we need them again?

Wife: Hahahahahahahahaha!

Once the kids have arrived on the scene and gotten old enough to pipe up asking for a new bike, wardrobe, Caribbean Disney cruise, or My First Large Hadron Collider, you need to rein in their assumptions that money grows not on trees but magically inside Dad's wallet and Mom's purse every night, kind of like a fungus backed by the Federal Reserve. This is often a special duty for dads. On the list of Daddy to-do's, "Teach Kids the Value of a Buck" is situated near the very top, right between "Don't Talk Back to Your Mother" and "Here's How to Play 'The Star-Spangled Banner' with Your Armpit."

Whether you're looking to introduce your children to the concept of spending wisely or you're desperate to save because you got laid off, have the money discussion with your kids in advance warns Lou Manza, professor of psychology at Lebanon Valley College in Pennsylvania.

"If something's been going on for months and months, sit the kids down beforehand and explain it to them," Manza says. "Don't just spring it on them in the car on the way to the store."

Tailor your financial discussion to the age, maturity, and temperament of your child, and focus on giving them choices and helping them feel that they have some control in the situation.

"You can make them understand that everyone needs to save, we're a family, and everybody helps out," Manza says. "You can tell them, 'Mom is cutting back like this, and Dad like this,' so it's not just the kid who's paying the price."

By the way, this strategy works with holidays and vacations, too. It might be difficult, but if you can adjust family expectations—starting, most importantly, with your own—you can teach some important lessons in financial responsibility. If you decide an expensive vacation isn't in the credit cards this year, get the whole family involved in planning your staycation. Set a budget and let each family member plan a day of outings. Or perhaps for the holidays you might all decide to concentrate your spending on one big family gift—such as a vacation—and forgo a pile of presents under the tree. Or the family can organize a garage sale together, the kids can opt to give up some of their allowance, or they can agree to cancel cable for a month or two, or whatever. Make a budget and a plan, cut back or redirect spending, do something to earn some extra money, and get everyone involved.

Whatever you do, don't say, "We're broke." That's only going to frighten the kids and is almost as bad as saying nothing (if you're worried about money, the kids will pick up on it). You don't want the kids to suddenly have visions of your family pushing a shopping cart down the alley. Instead, focus on the need to make choices about where your money goes and on having the kids learn to spend money wisely. It's important because kids often don't make the connection between the family budget and day-to-day spending. I'm not saying you have to break out last year's tax return before each shopping trip, but just that you want the kids (and maybe you, too) to understand that money is a finite resource, not something that automatically comes out of the wall at the bank.

Food and clothing

When it comes to your kids, you want to give them everything, but children will do just fine if they don't have the latest designer-label overcoat that they'll outgrow after one season. Up until the tween years, kids are pretty easy to shop for—it's basically whatever Mom or Dad picks out. Right now, Li'l Money could care less whether his shirts come from the thrift shop, though I'm sure that by his high school years he'll be demanding a $50 vintage T-shirt that's distressed just so that it looks like it came from . . . a thrift shop. The answer here is to give your kids a budget shortly before they start caring about clothes and let them start to make their own choices.

One approach is to give each kid a clothing allowance and guidelines about how many shirts, pants, and socks are needed, and what is or isn't acceptable for the school (or family) dress code. Beyond that, they can buy what they want. If they spend less, they can keep the money. If your budget is pinched, let the kids keep half of what they save, or some set amount, like $20, just as long as you give them an incentive to shop wisely. Conversely, if the kids want to spend more than the allowed amount, they have to come up with the difference on their own.

Before that happens, do your best to turn your kids into smart shoppers. Take them shopping with you so that they can see how many brand-new items end up in thrift and consignment stores. When Li'l Money was born, friends gave us some gorgeous larger-sized clothing for him to grow into, including one very handsome outfit with a sweater for trips up north at the holidays. By the time Christmas rolled around, however, the kid had already outgrown the clothes, and he certainly hadn't gotten a chance to wear them in the 90-degree heat of south Florida. Off to the thrift shop they went, still wrapped and tagged, much to the delight of some other bargain-hunting parent.

Also try to buy larger sizes when you can. My boy looked fine and was comfortable in a slightly oversized jacket that lasted from the fourth grade to the fifth. And when he was wearing size 6 shoes, we kept an eye out for any size 7s that were on sale rather than having to pay full price later on when his toes burst through his boots. When we find a good selection of $2 T-shirts on vacation, we get one the right size for now, two bigger ones for later.

With food, we've tried to keep him from getting too stuck on any one brand of anything so that we don't get a meltdown when, for example, he has to suffer the crushing indignity of eating store-brand cereal instead of Cheerios. Learning how to shop at grocery stores and stocking up when items are at their cheapest goes a long way with this kind of stuff, as I'll discuss in chapter 10. The one place we've failed is with strawberry milk. How the kid ever heard of it, I'll never know, but one day at the grocery store he spied a box of powdered strawberry milk mix and insisted he would die without it. We were happy to encourage him to drink milk, and when it became a regular item on the grocery list, we found the brand of strawberry-flavored powder that cost the least per serving.

That worked great until the grocery store started carrying premixed strawberry milk (curse you, Prairie Farms!) and the kid declared he would drink only that. Sometimes the strawberry milk is on sale, but usually it's a better buy to get the regular milk (which is often on sale) and throw in a dime's worth of strawberry powder. As any parent will tell you, arguing "It's the same thing!" won't get you too far with a kid who's made up his or her mind. And when my boy sets his opinion, it's locked down so tight that you'll actually hear the "doink-doink" sound from *Law & Order*.

But one of the few convenient things about kids is that when they're young, they go to bed before you do, and when they're older, they hole up in their rooms without the least interest in how Mom and Dad handle the domestic chores, as long as it doesn't involve them. So . . . the kid wasn't around, I was cleaning up in the kitchen, and I happened to have this empty jug from the premixed strawberry milk that he drained in world-record time. Who's to know if regular milk happens to get poured into it along with the cheaper strawberry-flavored powder? The same tactic can work with any of a kid's must-have ingestibles that come in a box, bottle, or tin. The bag of store-brand Chocolate Frosted Sugar Bombs cereal fits just fine into the box from the premium brand, too.

Okay, call me a coward. But hear me out. Veteran parents always say you've got to pick your battles, but that forces you into choosing between fighting or capitulating (by the way, "capitulating" is an SAT word he'll know later because I scrimped on strawberry milk now so we can afford a tutor in high school). Rather than choosing between being a Scrooge who puts his foot down or a wimp who caves into the child's demands, I choose instead to be Generous Dad, the great giver of all good things who miraculously makes it all fit into the family budget. Bait and switch is illegal only if the appliance store does it. Besides, this is strawberry-flavored milk. It's not like I'm swapping his 2010 Châteauneuf-du-Pape for some Two Buck Chuck.

Freeing up cash

With infants, your first stop should be a wholesale buying club such as Costco. The savings on formula (if you need it) and disposable diapers (if you go that way) will more than pay for the annual membership. Just don't get carried away with the awesome $1,200 stainless-steel backyard grilling "system" and blow your budget. Another option to consider is Amazon Mom (gender stereotyping much, Amazon?), which allows you to subscribe to regular deliveries of baby stuff at a discount. You save 5 percent with up to four deliveries a month, 15 percent with five or more. That cuts a box of 194 Pampers from 25 cents apiece to either 23 cents or 20 cents. Plus, you get free shipping and you can combine the Amazon Mom plan with Amazon Prime discounts as well. You may even be able to apply additional discounts, such as special offers from parenting magazines, to save more.

You can find a rundown on the whole strategy at BabyCheapskate .com. That site—and other baby discount sites, which unfortunately insist on focusing on moms—are another source for great deals. BabyCheapskate.com recently dug up a nice deal on the Little Tikes Cozy Coupe, the ubiquitous red-and-yellow toddler car that Li'l Money gravitated toward as if it were his destiny when he was two years old. His favorite part? The driver's door that opens and closes.

I once watched him get in and out of his Cozy Coupe more than forty times straight. We scored a great deal on one at a baby consignment store, and my advice is if you see one, grab it. As we walked out we endured the baleful, jealous stares of other parents. If you must buy new, hit the baby sites for a deal; but when your kid outgrows it, remember to get some of your dough back at the consignment store.

For other food and clothes, it comes down to how frugal you want or need to be. You can hit the farmers' market and make a month's worth of strained peas for less than half the cost of prepared baby food, or you can coupon like crazy and get a great deal at the store. There are more books and blogs about frugal living than I can begin to count, and you can glean good tips (and some crazy, extreme ones, too) from all of them. Using the grocery shopping approaches outlined in chapter 10 works for us, along with taking advantage of sales and outlet stores.

Making ends meet

You need to move from the convenient side of frugal to the side that requires more time and effort. Instead of an occasional trip to the consignment store, make a regular circuit of consignment and thrift shops as well as local garage sales. Babies and kids outgrow most clothes (except, in my experience, shoes) before they wear them out. Somehow, Li'l Money can pound through a pair of discount sneakers in a few scant months. Fortunately, he's not nearly as hard on his boots, so in our house winter lasts until Mother's Day. (Since we live in Michigan, that's not really much of stretch.)

Another source of clothing bargains is eBay, where moms tend to bundle up all the stuff a kid has outgrown and auction the whole lot. For $20 you can obtain an entire season's wardrobe if you're lucky, and anything that doesn't fit can be donated to the thrift store (take a picture, get a receipt, and take the tax deduction). You can similarly sell off what your kid has outgrown and cut the cost even more.

Swapping with other parents is another option, and you can find or organize a clothing swap through your neighborhood, church, community center, or school. Anything stained or excessively worn gets thrown out, of course, but the rest is up for trading; you swap one item for each one you bring. And you don't have to limit it to clothes, but can add baby blankets, maternity clothes, toys, and more. I've even seen swaps for unused Christmas decorations.

Pinching pennies so hard that Lincoln gets a headache

Go as frugal as you can. Start with any and all of the tips from Mary Hunt at EverydayCheapskate.com. Worn through an old pair of flannel pajama pants or shirt? Meet your new Swiffer pads. Dishes coming out of the dishwasher less than clean? Try cleaning out the sprayer-arm holes with a hanger instead of buying a new one for $500. And Mary's homemade laundry detergent recipe cuts your cost per load from 35 cents to 3 cents. Mary also has wonderful advice on living debt-free, so if that's one of your financial goals, you'll find her advice doubly helpful at the DebtFreeLiving.com site.

What is pretty much the bible for frugal living is Amy Dacyczyn's *Tightwad Gazette*. Long before the Internet, Dacyczyn published a newsletter filled with tips on how she and her husband raised a passel of kids on a $30,000 annual salary and managed to save $39,000 in seven years. Dacyczyn has retired as the country's leading penny-pinching publisher, but she collected the best of her advice in *The Complete Tightwad Gazette*. Check the library for a copy, or find a used or new copy online.[1]

If your income has taken a huge hit, check with your county

social services agencies and your church for programs that can help you and your family over the hump, and apply for any support programs you can. You've paid taxes all your life, and this is why. At this point in the postrecession landscape, nobody should feel any qualms about claiming whatever they can from the government they support. Food pantries, volunteer programs, and more are there to help people in just your situation. Apply for everything. I was stunned when the special kindergarten program my son went to gave us a partial scholarship, but we wouldn't have gotten it if we hadn't asked.

Most important, let your friends and extended family know what you need. You don't have to give people a full financial disclosure to let them know that things are tight. They've been tight for almost everyone the last few years, and my feeling is that it's made people more willing to share whatever extra they have. A friend of Mrs. Funny Money loves to shop estate sales and somehow wound up with a free canning pot. Now we enjoy the most wonderful homemade tomato sauce all winter long. A friend of a friend wanted to clear out a storage unit where he had a bunch of tile remnants and he offered us our pick. It transformed our ugly cement patio into a backyard retreat. And when my wife mentioned to a coworker that Li'l Money had joined the Cub Scouts, she provided us with the uniform her son had outgrown. Every dime you don't spend is a dime you have for something essential, so don't be shy.

In our case, cutting the food budget was a family effort that we took up later in The $1,000 Challenge, because by that time we were well beyond the years of formula and baby food. We also weren't spending a lot of money on clothing for Li'l Money, probably because the long-suffering Mrs. Funny Money already used all the tactics described here to keep the boy dressed at a discount. And, fortunately for us, he doesn't seem to be the kind of kid who's going to demand expensive boots, the latest sneakers, or designer-label goods when he gets to high school. That will just leave all the other teen costs, such as thousands for robot-design camp, driver's training, astronomical car insurance, and enough orthodontia to rival the front end of a '49 Buick.

School supplies

I've found that shopping for your kid's school supplies is one of those things that really needs to be done well in advance. Otherwise, all the other parents at work will get to the office supply closet ahead of you.

More importantly, back-to-school time is the first leg of the family's Triple Crown of debt. It starts when you don't plan, budget, or save for school supplies but, hey, Junior needs an Avengers backpack and Missy wants fourteen Hello Kitty notebooks, so, along with a bunch of clothes, it all goes on a credit card. You figure you'll pay it off in the next few months.

Then comes Christmas, the second leg of the debt Triple Crown, and, wham, you can't scrimp there because the kids are only young once, your wife deserves more than a little something for putting up with you all year, and it's your turn to host the holiday dinner, complete with mashed organic Brussels sprouts shaped like a turkey to keep your cousin happy, because she's now a vegan Wiccan who's actually celebrating the Feast of Ullr. The holidays are priceless, as they used to say in the MasterCard ads, and that's exactly how you will finance this one. But you'll be getting that tax refund check in time to wipe out your tab from December plus whatever stubborn debt is left from school shopping. Six months, tops, and you'll have that credit card balance back to zero.

But then it's off to the races once again, this time with summer vacation, the Belmont Stakes of the family debt circuit. This is the

year you promised your wife (who's still putting up with you) something special, and the kids have never had the chance to see the
Grand Canyon, the Czech Republic, or the Gowanus Canal. So . . .
out comes the credit card, and that new debt gets piled on top of the
Christmas and back-to-school spending, which, by the way, is just
around the corner—again.

Before you let the debt horses out of the gate, stop and do a little
planning in the fall. The big office supply stores and discount stores
start running all kinds of back-to-school specials well before September. (You'll know when that is, because it's about the time they
haul out the Christmas carols for the store sound systems.) With a
little planning you won't go broke, and you'll even get another chance
to school your kids in budgeting, shopping, and spending.

Freeing up cash

Start by going through all the stuff left from last year or that you
already have on hand. You'd be surprised at how much you can
winnow down your back-to-school shopping list if you get your kid
to realize that the centimeters on the ruler from fourth grade still
work in fifth grade. It's also a reason to dissuade little kids from
picking out a *Dora the Explorer* calculator that they'll be too embarrassed to use in middle school.

Having your student put some of his or her own money into the
back-to-school budget is a good idea, too, especially for discretionary items such as clothes or electronic gadgets, suggests Nina Sutton, author of *The Chic Mom's Guide to Feeling Fabulous*. Parents can
set up some quick and easy chores, such as having the kids clean
their rooms each night, so they can earn a portion of the money
already being budgeted before going shopping.

"If they're doing something to earn that money, they feel some responsibility for the purchases," Sutton says. For younger kids, sticking to the budget may be as simple as adding up purchases on their shopping lists and crossing off items. For older students, she suggests using gift cards to give them a feeling of control and responsibility. "With the gift card, they need to choose how they're going to spend it, but when it's done, it's done," Sutton says.

Making ends meet

Once you get your shopping list together, sit down with your kids and sort out needs versus wants. A youngster might be more willing to accept using last year's backpack and binder if it stretches the budget to cover Justin Bieber stickers for their locker. (Kids: we try to protect them with hand sanitizer and school-bus safety belts, when what they really need to be shielded from is their own bad taste.)

At the beginning of August, start keeping an eye out for back-to-school specials, such as 10-for-$1 pencils or notebooks, which may show up at the supermarket or drugstore just as often as at discount and office supply stores. As a person who still works at and reads an actual printed newspaper, let me point out that the ad inserts in the Sunday edition are your best bet for finding and comparing offers (also, your hands absorb a special ingredient from newspaper ink that helps prevent gum disease). Last fall, for example, two of the big office supply stores advertised free backpacks with a $10 purchase of other school items.

Parents with fashion-conscious kids might want to hold back some of the budget for their clothing and just buy one or two outfits for the start of school. That way, the kids can shop the clearance sales later, and, if their classmates are sporting some hot new look that your kids missed, they can fill in any wardrobe gaps later, instead of buying clothes they may not end up wearing.

Beyond teaching money management and shopping skills, parents can use back-to-school time for lessons in applied math, whether it's subtraction and addition for first graders or calculating and comparing the per-unit cost of a $3 bag of ten pens versus a $4.25 package that holds twenty-four.

Pinching pennies so hard that Lincoln gets a headache

Between reusing leftover items from previous years and shaving your shopping list down to the basics, try to cover the essentials but leave maybe two or three new things that the kids can get—within reason. Ask around to see if your friends and other parents can fill in the gaps. In my case, I've received enough press releases and financial studies stuffed into ring binders that I could outfit Li'l Money's entire class. If tenth-grade math requires a particular model of graphing calculator, for example, you can try eBay or Craigslist, but chances are that there are plenty of those gizmos gathering dust in the homes of any eleventh graders you know. Your kid's older friends (or their parents) will be glad to part with their old one for a few bucks.

For more help, check with local social service agencies and your church. Since the recession, I've found several companies and charities giving away school supplies, and my own church, the very generous and wonderful First Presbyterian Church of Birmingham, collects school supplies to distribute to folks who need to spend their money elsewhere. Check with your nearest United Way, and also search on the Web for a school supply giveaway event in your area. They often take place in July, so, again, start looking earlier than the week before school starts.

Once again, I couldn't find a lot of savings in this category, because we were already pretty good at keeping costs low. Mrs. Funny

Money picked up a sturdy Lands' End backpack on sale for about $14, and it's lasted four years with no signs of giving out. It's in the boy's favorite color rather than being adorned by some kid-TV abomination such as Barney, the evil off-key, brain rotting dinosaur even kids loathe by third grade, so Li'l Money doesn't gripe about using it year after year.

The big surprise is how many of his school supplies can be reused from year to year. The trick is to dig through the whole lot at the end of the school year, figure out what can be kept for next year, and then put it all safely away so that the glue sticks, crayons, and scissors don't go AWOL over the summer or get dragged out to the sandbox. And if the kid insists on brand-new pencils next fall, he can pick any box he wants at the dollar store.

Health care

When you have children you lose not just your sanity, sex life, and car keys but your vocabulary as well. This explains why otherwise sophisticated professionals excuse themselves from business meetings to "go potty" and conclude phone conversations with "buhbye." Adult conversation is even more fractured in our house because, as I mentioned earlier, Li'l Money is a late-talker.

Late talking is a little like dyslexia for the ears, but he has made astounding progress with language, thanks to lots of effort, patience, and unreimbursed speech therapy. But as a toddler, the confusing communications dragged out potty training to the point where I thought he wouldn't be out of Pampers until I was in Depends. But when the boy got the knack of using the bathroom he embraced the concept with gusto. When nature called on the then-four-year-old kid one day at the home improvement store, I turned to lead him to the men's room, only to find him up on a platform of plumbing items—planted in front of a $400 designer toilet that soon would no longer be for display purposes only.

I managed to avoid paying for that pricey porcelain, which would have come on top of the average of $815 a year Michigan families with special-needs kids spend on out-of-pocket costs. In our case, that includes out-of-state specialists and consultants, plus private speech and reading therapy, plus a $190-an-hour special education attorney to keep our local school system from making the common—but extremely harmful—mistake of pushing a late talker into autism programs.

None of it comes cheap, and none of it is covered by insurance. But there is one place I found a break: taxes. Setting up a flexible spending account to cover $4,000 of our medical expenses took that money right off the top of my salary, reducing my taxable income and my tax bill. The money is deducted from each paycheck and added to a special account. I then file health care claims against the account, and I'm reimbursed tax-free. At our tax rates, that knocked an even $1,200 off our projected tax tab to Uncle Sam for the year, according to the handy-dandy IRS withholding calculator.[2] The same break applies to the Michigan state income tax, which cut $174 off our state tax bill, for a total of $114.50 in monthly savings, which shows up in each paycheck after my withholding was adjusted.

While the tax break certainly helps, it doesn't completely solve the problem, since what we get back on taxes is only about 30 percent of the money we put out. Michigan, like many other states, now requires insurance companies to pay for autism therapies, but that leaves families like mine, with kids who have other developmental issues, on our own. Still, we muddle through. My wife became particularly adept at interpreting Li'l Money's requests, explaining, "He says it's time for the playground," when I asked, "Why does he want to put socks on the pumpkin?"

Although he sometimes still uses just two or three words when other kids use two or three sentences, Li'l Money gets his message across. After working late one night and missing the chance to tuck him in, I sat with my coffee the next morning as he trundled out of bed. He shuffled over in his pajamas and threw his arms around me. "Luv," he declared as he put his head on my shoulder.

I don't get it. If he's the one with few words, how come I'm the one left speechless?

Freeing up cash

The good news is that most companies with any kind of decent benefits program offer a flexible spending health care account. The bad news is that you can shelter only $2,500 a year now. This hits families like mine that shell out a lot for health care during the year, but the fact is that most people using a flex account set aside quite a bit less.

Comparison shopping when benefits enrollment time comes around in the fall is another way to see if you can save. Co-pays on medical visits and prescriptions seem to go up every year, along with the deductible. If your workplace offers more than one option, don't just automatically renew your plan every year, but consider how your qualified health care spending in the past year would fit into all the options and lower your costs. Or, if your spouse has a health plan, compare the plans to see which works best for you at the lowest cost.

If you're using a flex account, remember the one big caveat: you need to spend all the money during the calendar year or you lose it. So base your withholding on your actual medical spending, which is another good reason to track your spending and maintain a budget.

Making ends meet

Start shopping aggressively for all your health care spending, from prescriptions to health plans. Talk to your doctor, pharmacist, and any therapists or service providers and ask them how you can save, especially if you're going without insurance.

If you've lost insurance because you lost your job, you're probably eligible for COBRA, an acronym for a federal law that gives you sixty days to continue your health coverage by picking up the entire premium yourself. COBRA covers spouses and kids, as well as people who lose insurance because of divorce, a reduction in hours at work, if you got too old to stay on your parents' policy, or if you were on a relative's policy when that person became old enough to switch to Medicare.

COBRA isn't usually an affordable option if you lost a job, because the premium you paid as an employee was likely less than a third, or even a fifth, of the total cost your employer was paying. Private coverage, on average, will cost less than half of what you'll pay for COBRA. One tactic is to shop for private insurance, and mix and match private and COBRA coverage, using COBRA for those family members who can't get comparable, affordable private coverage.

If you do go with COBRA but are working to land a new job and the benefits it brings, consider this free trick for filling the COBRA gap. You have sixty days to decide whether to sign up for COBRA, and another forty-five days to pay your first premium. If you get hit with a major medical expense in those sixty days, you can opt in to COBRA and be covered retroactively, and you still have more than a month to come up with the first premium payment.

If you've got a side job, moonlight, or work as a freelancer, look for health care coverage through trade groups and professional associations, or see if you can get group coverage as a small business.

Fourteen states let you qualify as a "group of one" for group rates,[3] and all states allow you to qualify with two employees. If your wife maintains the Web page for your freelance yak-grooming business, see if you can set things up to qualify. Naturally, there will be hoops to jump through, and there will be plenty of red tape, because, you know, insurance. Another option is short-term gap insurance policies covering only catastrophic illnesses and accidents. Call several insurance agents and compare options. A good guide to the basics of buying your own health insurance is at www.insure.com.[4]

Pinching pennies so hard that Lincoln gets a headache

As always, free is better than cheap, so start with any options you can find for free health care for your kids (and you). If you're out of work, start with all the social service agencies and government programs such as Medicaid and the Children's Health Insurance Program, even though it will be frustrating and often feel like a waste of time. Your local United Way is also a good source. Again, this is why you and your family paid taxes all those years and why you made that $20 weekly paycheck deduction to United Way. (Make a note to yourself that when you do get back to work, you'll contribute again.)

For typical care, check out walk-in clinics, urgent care centers, and even the health care options increasingly provided by Target and some of the big drugstore chains. Need to check your blood pressure? Skip the $60 cuff and regularly stop at Walgreens and use the free machine instead. When it comes to prescriptions, a limited number of commonly prescribed drugs are available from Kroger, Target, Meijer, Food City, and other big chains. Let your doctor know that you want lower-priced generics rather than more expensive brand-name drugs, or ask if you can substitute an over-the-counter remedy. If you're facing a co-pay on prescriptions, ask your doctor for a ninety-day prescription instead of thirty days, or for pills at double the dose that you can cut in half (say, 500 mg instead of 250 mg), or both, to stretch your time between paying for refills. Also check out the Partnership for Prescription Assistance,[5] which aims to helps people without prescription drug coverage, and NeedyMeds,[6] which lists programs to help you find discounted medications.

When it comes to tests, remind your doctor that you're paying out of pocket and ask if each one is really necessary or can be postponed. With treatments, ask to pay Medicare rates (which are lower) or if your doctor's practice offers a sliding scale of fees based on income. Look for a community center that offers free or low-cost medical services,[7] and check out other low-cost insurance options at healthcare.gov. The National Association of Free and Charitable Clinics lists free and charitable clinics.[8] Also check out medical centers and teaching hospitals near you.

In many cases, doctors can get you free samples, so let them know that you're in a tight situation. I had one physician who made it a point to stockpile a ridiculous quantity of samples in a closet that looked like it contained an entire Rite Aid. He wouldn't have cared if I drove a gold-plated Mercedes, and he routinely handed out a full course of sample drugs to treat an infection or rash.

If you end up needing a medical procedure and you're paying for it yourself, do some comparison shopping. The cost of services varies widely even within a small area. Many states require hospitals to post their rates, and other hospitals voluntarily do so. Search online for "hospital pricing" in your state. In Michigan, for example, many hospitals participate in listing rates online.[9] In Metro Detroit, the average charge for delivering a baby ranges from more than $14,000 at one hospital to less than $6,000 at another. In addition, contact a hospital ombudsman or patient representative to discuss charges and payment assistance plans beforehand.

It'll take some digging and hassle and lots of phone calls, so be prepared, but it's better than letting your kid go without care. I never expected that we would qualify for a partial scholarship in the preschool speech therapy program Li'l Money attended, either because there were lots of folks worse off than we were or because the program would have been oversubscribed. But somehow we did, and the boy got the help he needed without too much of a hit to our budget.

It still remains to be seen how access to health care and its cost will change under the Affordable Care Act, which is still rolling out health exchanges in several states along with other incentives and limits on health care costs. Focus on your needs, keep an eye out for new information, and ask lots and lots of questions.

The Bottom Line

Goal: $1,000

Week 1—Transportation . . . $41.61
Week 2—Miscellaneous . . . $132.89
Week 3—Utilities . . . $139.39
Week 4—Kid Costs . . . $114.50
Total monthly savings . . . $428.39

Left to cut . . . $571.61

We already were pretty frugal with food, clothes, and school supplies for Li'l Money, but the tax move to run our speech therapy and health care expenses through a flexible health spending account put me over the $100 goal in this category, for a total of $428.39 in cuts. That left $571.61 still to cut to make my $1,000 goal.

As for teaching Li'l Money important life lessons about money, he's become a very good saver, if an impatient one. Although he's quick to exclaim, "I can save the money!" when he sees something he wants, the reality that it'll take four or five weeks of allowance isn't met with the same enthusiasm. I often make him a countdown calendar so he can tick off the days and feel like he's making progress, even if he's just waiting for next week's allowance.

What's more interesting is how many money lessons my boy has reinforced for me and Mrs. Funny Money. Babies show up and somehow, magically, the family budget stretches to accommodate cribs, diapers, and the collected works of Elmo, all to the tune of hundreds of dollars a month. What's astonishing is that the same parents would have sworn they couldn't save anywhere near that amount a year before the kid was born. Sure, the budget stretches hard, but it rarely snaps. The late songwriter Bill Morrissey once put it succinctly, "There's Bud in the 'fridge instead of Becks/And I ain't seen any side effects."

Likewise, a walk through the toy store with Li'l Money becomes a lasting lesson in the dangers of instant gratification at any age. Just as it becomes obvious that you're going to go broke $3.99 at a time right there in the Hot Wheels aisle, it sinks in to the parental consciousness that you also can go broke $39.99 at a time down at the mall. Later, when you notice that the T-shirt that fit the boy just fine two months ago now barely reaches below his neck, you suddenly realize that tomorrow does come. Suddenly a future of scout camp, driver's ed, college, and his wedding day are breathing down my neck, along with the realization that if he's getting older, I might be, too. That's about the time I switched my little guy's bedtime story from *The Runaway Bunny* to dramatic readings from my 401(k) prospectus.

When I put it all together—budgeting, expense reduction, deferred spending, and long-term savings—I'd say my little boy has given me a pretty good financial education in a few short years. And when it comes to teaching his old man the value of a buck? Let's just say that 99-cent margarita I bought Mrs. Funny Money all those years ago was the best investment I ever made.

6

Work Expenses

Yes, There's the Expense of Parking and a Work
Wardrobe, but Don't Overlook the Never-
Ending Psychic Costs Inflicted by ABBA

The whole point of working is to make money, but it turns out that holding a job is a pretty expensive proposition.

There's the cost of your work clothes, your commute to work, lunch, and parking, plus intangibles, such as the cost to your self-esteem when it's groveling time before the boss and the cost to your sanity when your nearest coworker spends hours mumbling along to her downloads of ABBA's greatest hits. (I don't care how many Volvos or how much Absolut vodka they send us, the Swedes can never undo that damage.)

But when I went to trim my work-related spending for my next installment of The $1,000 Challenge, most of those expenses didn't show up. Commuting costs were part of auto expenses; lunch and clothing came out of my personal spending; and the Xanax co-pays fell under the medical category.

My only big work-related costs were several newspaper subscriptions, including Detroit's finest broadsheet, professional journalism reviews, and child care for Li'l Money. Mrs. Funny Money was working three days a week, with two afternoon shifts that over-lapped with my work hours, so our roster of sitters could rack up to six hours a day. That's an average of $126 a week to keep the kid from ingesting a week's supply of Teddy Grahams or flushing the dining room drapes. Then there were the additional costs of care during school breaks and summer vacation, including added hours for the sitters and day-camp fees.

The five newspapers we get every day at my house would seem like a tempting target for cost cutting, especially when you consider that some national publications, such as *The Wall Street Journal*, can cost more than $300 a year. But my mother didn't have any children dumb enough to become a newspaper columnist who writes about what a great idea it is to cancel your newspaper subscriptions. (And remember, a special ingredient in newsprint ink gets absorbed through your hands and helps prevent gum disease!) So finding any savings in the work-expense category meant I was going to have to focus on the costs of tending to Li'l Money or finding ways to make my commute cheaper.

Professional expenses

Whether it's tools or uniforms for your job, professional education requirements, training, journal subscriptions, union dues, or park-ing, cutting this category isn't going to give you much wiggle room. The best I can suggest is to make sure you take all the tax breaks you can find, try to get some costs covered by your employer, take advantage of discounts, and cut out as much as you can.

Freeing up cash

As long as they equal 2 percent of my adjusted gross income, I can deduct the cost of all those newspaper subscriptions and professional journals as a work-related business expense, which I already did. In fact, you can deduct several work-related costs, such as professional association dues, work expenses that you aren't reimbursed for, and even a home office if you are required to maintain one (be careful, though, as the IRS has gotten very picky about this one, and it can mark you as audit-bait). You also can write off job-related educational expenses, job-search expenses, tools and supplies, work uniforms, and depreciation on a computer required for work. If you travel between offices, you can deduct that expense, but not your normal commuting costs. In some cases, you can even deduct business gifts and entertainment. Check the IRS.gov Web site for details,[1] because there are very specific rules and limits, or consult a tax professional. You have to itemize to claim these deductions, which will be more effort if you usually file a short form or EZ tax return and, if you pay someone to prepare you taxes, that will cost more.

Making ends meet

For things like professional journals, association memberships, and the like, see if you can expense those items at work. Instead of getting a small tax deduction, that'll save you the entire amount. One approach is to find out whether your professional association will discount group memberships. For example, one of my journalism societies offers bulk memberships to newspapers that sign up all of their eligible members, which also gives the paper a break on entering the society's annual journalism contest, since only members can enter. Even if your employer doesn't want to bear the cost, you can reimburse them and get the lower group rate.

You can look for professional publications at the library or split the cost of subscriptions with coworkers. Anything that is available online is easy to share, or you can have anything that's still printed sent to the office. Or, if your company is doing okay, ask your boss to cover the cost of a subscription.

Pinching pennies so hard Lincoln gets a headache

Eliminate whatever you can, of course. If you're still in school, look for educational discounts on student memberships or subscriptions. At some professional workshops, students, interns, and others may be able to trade working at the registration desk or helping set up the event for discounted or free registration.

While you should deduct any and all professional expenses you can, if your income is low enough, you can also claim additional tax benefits through the Earned Income Tax Credit. Aimed at low-income wage earners, the EITC could have put up to $5,891 in your pocket after filing your 2012 tax return. The idea is that the costs of working, including child care and transportation, can eat up so much of a paycheck that low-income workers would make more money on public assistance or simply can't afford to work, so this tax credit bolsters their paychecks. Workers who earn less than $50,270 annually may be eligible for the credit, which averaged $2,200 in 2011. A small credit is available even if you don't have children. About two dozen states also offer their own version of the Earned Income Tax Credit, so check your state tax information, too. (Michigan recently killed our state EITC so we could cut business taxes, because, you know, it's more important to help the corporations that underpay their workers so much that their employees qualify as "the working poor.")

If you haven't heard about the EITC, or mistakenly think you won't qualify, you're not alone. A study by the New America Foundation found that in California alone during 2009, an estimated 800,000 Californians missed $1.2 billion in EITC refunds, an average of $1,400 per family. Overall, one-fifth of all families that qualify for the credit fail to claim it.

The best part is that the EITC is a refundable tax credit. Most tax deductions just knock down part of your overall tax bill. A refundable credit, however, actually prompts the government to send you a check. This credit gets overlooked by a lot of low-income parents who don't need to file a return. (If you qualify and haven't claimed the credit in past years, you can amend your past tax returns for up to three years or file a claim for past years and get a tidy windfall.)

You can estimate the amount of your tax credit at eitcoutreach .org[2] and check your eligibility by using the EITC Assistant from the IRS.[3] This isn't the easiest thing to claim, so get free tax help from the IRS.gov Web site, by calling your local 211 or 311 community information service, or from a tax preparation volunteer. Between January and April, the IRS Volunteer Income Tax Assistance program offers free tax help, which you can find by going to the IRS Web site[4] or by calling 800-906-9887. Older taxpayers can also get help from the Tax Counseling for the Elderly and AARP Foundation's Tax Aide programs at aarp.org[5] or by calling 888-227-7669.

For myself, the only savings I get on professional expenses is a group membership to one business journalism society at work and whatever I can deduct on my taxes. The savings equals whatever your marginal tax rate is, so in my case it's about 25 cents on every dollar. Since I already claimed those deductions, it wasn't going to add to my cost cutting for this project. That meant finding any savings in the work-expense category was going to have to focus on commuting (which I already tackled in chapter 2) or the costs of tending to the young 'un.

Commuting

I already focused on the costs of cars, insurance, and so on earlier, so I won't spend a lot of time going over the same ground, but you can't escape the fact that the biggest use most of us make of our vehicles is getting back and forth to work. As more Americans have moved out to the suburbs for schools, the two-car family has become a necessity, especially since both parents usually have to work to afford higher-priced suburban housing.

Freeing up cash

Consider this: based on AAA's national average of 59.6 cents per mile, you're paying $298 a year for each mile you drive to work, assuming you commute five days a week for fifty weeks a year. Plus, the farther away you work, the more hours of child care you need. My daily commute costs an estimated $8,882 a year, at 59.6 cents per mile, plus other costs, such as parking and tolls. Add Mrs. Funny Money's three-day-a-week commute and it's another $5,329. All together, our after-tax cost of going back and forth to work is more than $14,000 a year.

Anything that you can do to shorten your commute—or eliminate it entirely—is going to save you money (and probably cut your child care costs, too). That includes working flexible hours such as four days a week instead of five, even if that's not every week. If there's a branch or satellite office closer to home, see if you can move your job there instead of doing it at the faraway downtown headquarters. Even if your boss is one of those "out-of-sight, out-of-mind" Neanderthals, maybe he'll go for two days a week, which will still save you some dough. And, of course, if your job (and, more important, your boss, Mr. Cave Dweller) will allow you to work from home for even one or two days a week, that will also make a very nice dent in your job-related costs.

Making ends meet

You know, modern Americans just don't get to know one another the way our ancestors did back in the olden days, when they crossed the frontier in wagon trains, raised barns together, and used dial-up modems. One way to reclaim that old-timey community spirit is carpooling.

Once you've cut down the cost of driving by yourself as much as possible, look at the possibility of driving with other people who will share the cost of gas, tolls, and parking. If you can't arrange a car pool or ride-share, fire up the Interwebs and see if you can find car pool listings for your county, or a ride-matching service, often through your county or state transportation departments.

The downside, of course, is that every so many weeks you're going to be riding in Tracie's minivan, inhaling Cheerios dust while she blasts ABBA. Probably "Dancing Queen." Oh, who am I kidding? It's Tracie; of *course* it will be "Dancing Queen." Just grin and bear it, or pack one or two of those airline-size Absolut vodkas.

Pinching pennies so hard that Lincoln gets a headache

Here in mass-transit-impaired Motown, alternatives to the car are approached with general suspicion (as well as torches and pitchforks). If the Good Lord wanted us to walk, my hometown says, he would have given us wheels instead of feet. But if mass transit is a likelier option where you live, check to see if your employer offers a discount on monthly passes. Otherwise, ask if your employer offers

Qualified Transportation Benefits, also called a Commuter Savings Account or a Commuter Expense Reimbursement Account.

This works like a health care or dependent care savings account, allowing you to shelter $245 a month for public transportation (including a van pool) and/or $245 monthly for parking. You can have both types of accounts if, for example, you take a train and use a park-and-ride lot, but you can only use the parking account for parking expenses, and the transit account for mass transit costs.

In some cases employers provide public transit passes or even arrange a van pool service as a fringe benefit, and the value of these will be tax-free to you, which is an even better deal, since you're not paying and not being taxed on the benefit, either. At the very least you eliminate taxes on the money you pay for your commute, which boosts your take-home pay. This is a workplace benefit, so check with your personnel office. Your employer can also give you $20 per month, tax-free, to cover expenses for bicycle commuting.

Also check with your local social service agencies and charities to see if you can get commuting assistance, such as discount mass transit passes. Some areas even have programs to offer emergency aid for automobile costs, such as title fees and insurance.

Child care

It's tempting for two working parents to just keep working as usual and line up day care, but this can result in the family budget taking a big hit, with the child care tab eating up much of one parent's salary. This is the conundrum that many families face: working to pay a day-care bill that eats up all the wages from working. It also poses another question: Why bother having kids if you're not going to be around to raise them?

This issue was conveniently solved for the Funny Money family by the 2001 recession and "jobless" (at least for me) recovery that followed the tech-stock meltdown and the September 11 terrorist attacks. I had just finished a fellowship at Columbia University and, thanks to the bursting of the Internet bubble, wound up with no job at my previous employer, an online company whose stock slumped to around 60 cents a share (of course, I was holding thousands of shares, to boot). An offer to manage three daily business newspapers was then frozen during Mrs. Funny Money's first trimester. So, back in Florida, I ended up as a stay-at-home freelancing dad, assisted by Grandpa Verne.

We did eventually put Li'l Money in day care, mostly because, as an only child, he needed to go play with other kids. Still, I treasure my time as a stay-at-home dad, even if it does include one landmark diaper changing after the boy somehow ingested what must have been a jar of Gerber Strained Rancid Skunk Spleens. I think we had to repaint the ceiling after that one, and the room may have briefly been declared an EPA Superfund site.

Eventually my freelance income picked up and our budget leveled off, but with much fewer extras than during the B.C. (before child) era. That all changed when we moved to Detroit and the combination of Li'l Money's special education needs and the Great Recessepression walloped my wife's opportunities to work.

The annual cost of child care averages anywhere from about $4,600 in Mississippi to nearly $15,000 in Massachusetts for an infant in a child care center, according to Child Care Aware, while the cost of caring for a four-year-old in a home-based child care facility ran from about $4,100 in South Carolina to around $9,600 in New York. For a school-aged child in my current home state of Michigan, the study found the cost ranged from $3,500 to $4,500.

How any one family handles child care is a custom job, depending on location, resources, family members, school options, and the needs of the kids themselves. Things get a bit easier once all the offspring are in school, but that still leaves you with the question of how to care for and supervise them during summer vacations, winter breaks, and teacher-training days. Here in the suburbs of Wimpy Acres Estates, Mrs. Funny Money and I have even been forced to scramble for child care when school was canceled because of "freezing fog." Yes, that is a real thing, and it drove my Florida-bred wife nuts, especially after school had been canceled the week before on account of "heavy frost." She spluttered, "What's next for you oh-so hardy winter-loving Michiganians? Closing school because of excessive dew?"

Freeing up cash

If you've got child care arrangements in place that keep everybody feeling safe, happy, and relatively unstressed, let me say that this is the last part of your budget where you want to do even the smallest amount of tinkering. Also, please buy my next lottery ticket. If you're paying $500 a week for day care, you certainly want to shop around, but tread carefully. In my experience, it's likely that your perfect arrangements only last so long until the nanny gets married, the day-care center closes, or the baby-sitter gets accepted to State U (Mostly) Normal College.

The fastest way to savings on child care is another very valuable tax dodge: the dependent care credit. This allows you to claim a credit of 20 to 35 percent of expenses up to $3,000 for one kid who is thirteen or younger, $6,000 for two or more, as long as that care is necessary for you to work (or you and your spouse, if you file jointly). The credit shrinks as you make more money. The range is from $600 for higher-income taxpayers with one kid to $2,100 for two or more in a household with a lower adjusted gross income.

The credit also applies to any other dependent, including a spouse who, according to the IRS, "is physically or mentally incapable of self-care" and lives with you for at least half the year. (Ladies, the fact that, left to his own devices, your husband would wear the same socks for a week and subsist on a diet of Budweiser and Funyuns while zoning out to reruns of *Ice Road Truckers* doesn't count as "incapable of self-care," although it's an argument I would love to see play out in tax court.)

You can deduct payments for child care made to some relatives, but not your spouse, another dependent, one of the kid's parents, or another one of your progeny younger than nineteen. You also can deduct payments for summer day camp (but not sleep-away camp) if you send the kids there so you can go to work. And, obviously, you and your spouse need to have earned income since the whole point of the credit is to allow parents to go to work.

There's just one little catch: to claim this credit you are going to need to name names (and taxpayer IDs) when it comes to your child care provider(s), so if you have a private sitter or nanny, you'll be outing anyone who gets paid off the books. If you pay more than $1,800 a year to most caregivers, you qualify as a household employer and need to pay Social Security and Medicare taxes of 7.65 percent, while your sitter faces a 5.65 percent tax. If you pay more than $1,000 in any quarter, you also need to pay a 0.6 percent unemployment tax, plus any state taxes.

On wages of $2,300, for example, your share of the Social Security and Medicare taxes comes to $176 and your sitter pays $130, for a total of $306 plus whatever state and federal unemployment tax you may owe. If your marginal federal tax rate is 25 percent, a dependent care tax credit on $2,300 is worth $575. So, if you pay both chunks of the taxes, you're still ahead by $269. Adjust your tax withholding and you can redirect that $22.41 a month toward retirement savings, debt reduction, or other financial goals. Plus, you'll have the nice warm feeling that comes from doing your patriotic tax duty while also spending quality time with IRS Forms

W-2, W-3, 2441, Schedule H, and either Form 944 or 943. And when President Obama calls, your lack of "nanny-tax" offenses will send your nomination sailing right through the Senate so you can become our new ambassador to the Pacific Island commonwealth of Tuvalu. (It's sinking, so pack your snorkel, ambassador.)

If that's all too much hassle, consider a dependent care savings account. This operates much like the health care flexible spending account I employed for big savings in chapter 5. It's a benefit from your employer, included in most decent benefit plans, that allows you to shelter up to $5,000 from taxes per family (or $2,500 if you're married filing separately). The money is deducted from your regular paycheck and you file claims to get reimbursed tax-free. Also like a health care flex account, you have to use the money up by the end of the calendar year, and then file claims by a certain deadline, or you lose any unclaimed money. And, like with the dependent care tax credit, you have to identify your care providers, which can mean paying nanny taxes. You also can't pay a nonworking spouse to look after your own kids, and you need to have earned income.

In many cases the spending account will be a better deal than the tax credit, especially if you have a higher income and pay more than the tax credit's $3,000 (or $6,000) expense cap for child care during the year. You can't claim the same expenses for the tax credit if you've paid them under a dependent care spending account, but you can use a double-play strategy. If you pay $7,000 in child care expenses each year, shelter $5,000 in the spending account, then claim the tax credit against the remaining $2,000.

You can find a very cool interactive, printable worksheet from the FSAFEDS program of the U.S. Office of Personnel Management that calculates how you'll do with either a dependent care savings account or tax credit at fsafeds.com.[6]

Making ends meet

Let's get a little radical here and think about why you work: to make money, right? So, after the cost of child care (plus your commute and other expenses), do you?

Take the case of Mrs. Funny Money. Between the costs of her three days of commuting and two or three days of child care every week, it takes the first $11,000 of her salary for us to break even on her work-related expenses. If she were to get a $20,000 salary, that's only $9,000 gross, or $525 a month after taxes. Admittedly, that's using the official commuting cost of 59.6 cents per mile, and our actual out-of-pocket expenses for gas are less than that, but we do tend to overlook the increased maintenance, insurance, and wear and tear on the second car. Still, it's a good exercise to ask whether she couldn't make $9,000 closer to or even working from home, which would lower the cost of working, make one of the cars last longer, lower our taxable income (and possibly our tax rate), and still leave us with the same net amount of cash every month.

I did exactly this shortly after Li'l Money was born. I was offered a job writing investment analysis in the faraway office of a financial services firm. The salary was $55,000, which sounded impressive to an unemployed stay-at-home dad, but the costs of day care near that office, tolls on Florida's Turnpike, and gas for a lengthy commute each way reduced it to about $24,000, or $2,000 a month before taxes. There were also additional quality-of-life considerations, such as having to load my baby boy in the car at 7 a.m. and not getting him back home until at least 6 p.m., not the least of which would have been Daddy's lifelong debilitating guilt.

I took my quandary to a successful freelancing friend who assured me that I could build up my own independent writing to the same income level, so I turned down the job and gladly stayed home with my boy. It took nine months to start generating an average income of $2,000 a month, and some years I did even better.

I worked with one dad who found a more novel approach to the child care issue. After his daughter was born, he shifted to a night job while his wife worked days. This reduced their baby-sitting costs and increased the parents' involvement with the baby. They had just a slight overlap in their work schedules during the late afternoon, when they hired a sitter for about ninety minutes between the time he left for work and his wife arrived home.

Pinching pennies so hard that Lincoln gets a headache

For child care, shop around for providers who may offer a scholarship or fees on a sliding scale for families who've taken a hit to their income. Most state social service departments and early childhood foundations offer subsidies to low-income parents, too. Also check with your company; larger firms may negotiate a discount with a recommended day-care facility nearby as an employee benefit. If your company doesn't, maybe now is the time to gather up some signatures from other working parents and petition the benefits department to add discount day care.

Another option that might be cheaper with preschool kids is to find out if your school system offers half-day prekindergarten for four-year-olds. Even if it's not free, it can be cheaper than day care. Military families, including active and deployed members of the National Guard and reserves, should check with Operation Military Child Care about child care subsidies. Contact Child Care Aware at 800-424-2246 or at childcareaware.org.[7] Churches, youth organizations, and community centers also offer child care and after-school programs that may give you more affordable options. Don't forget to check with your local colleges, which often run very nice day-care options for their own staff or as part of teacher training and offer unused slots to the public, for a charge. Or you may be able to look for qualified sitters among student teachers or those studying child development.

If you can find a few like-minded neighbors, coworkers, or others, consider setting up a day-care cooperative, where several families hire one nanny or sitter to look after a small group of children. The care provider can get a good income while each individual pays less or can contribute time, materials, or space for the project. You'll need to set up everything in writing, appoint one parent (not the whole gang) to negotiate with and supervise the care provider, and set rules about how much notice any parent must give before pulling out of the co-op to keep one or two members from suddenly getting stuck bearing the entire cost.

If you've got any relatives who can help out, even one or two days a week, see whether they can be coaxed into action. Maybe an aunt can be the responsible adult on hand with the kids, with a neighbor or student hired as a mother's helper to assist with any strenuous chores (or DEFCON 1 stinky diapers). Between family, subsidies, community groups, and friends and neighbors, you can try to cobble together a plan that offers alternatives to writing a big day-care check every week. It'll take some research and phone calls and include some hassles. Plus you'll need a couple of backup plans, since the more moving parts your solution has, the more likely it is that problems will crop up.

Between my working at home, Grandpa Verne, and a few hours a day at a reasonably priced local day-care facility, we had better, more affordable care for Li'l Money than if I'd taken that full-time job. When my freelance work increased, I made more money than I would have working for someone else. There were days Grandpa or Li'l Money took ill and my work schedule got shot to hell for the day, so I'd make it up by working after the boy was in bed. The hassle factor was much higher, but so was my income, and, more important, I got to spend time caring for my son instead of stuck in traffic. And I'm almost fully recovered after the Toxic Diaper from Hell, except for a couple of bald spots on my eyebrows.

The Bottom Line

Goal: $1,000

Week 1—Transportation . . . $41.61
Week 2—Miscellaneous . . . $132.89
Week 3—Utilities . . . $139.39
Week 4—Kid Costs . . . $114.50
Week 5—Work Expenses . . . $90
Total monthly savings . . . $518.39

Left to cut . . . $481.61

Trimming our child care costs presented a tough balancing act. If we cut back on their hours too much, the best sitters would have dropped the Funny Money family. I needed sitters smart enough to help a kid with special needs through his homework, not some tween girls giving him plot points to the latest *Twilight* installment.

Child care is always a gnarly problem, with no easy or dependable solutions. But in this case the answer is simple: Dad.

Since I'm a reporter, there's some leeway in my schedule, but too often I let work slip into the evening when it isn't strictly necessary. Starting work earlier or taking a nondeadline story home would shave an hour or more off each day's baby-sitting tab. That saves some real money over the course of a month without making a big cut in the hours for our sitters. And I get to escape from any co-workers still tunelessly humming along to "Dancing Queen."

Some planning and hustle to get home so that the sitters put in only eight hours a week reduced our child care costs by $30 a week. I figured I could do that three weeks a month, so that if one night Federal Reserve chairman Ben Bernanke is trapped in a runaway balloon, I can work late and we'll still save $90 a month.

It wasn't quite the $100 I was aiming for, but with the extra savings I'd piled up in the previous weeks, I still brought the five-week total to $518.39, beating the $100-per-week goal for the project.

Of course, keeping the baby-sitters' hours low will mean rearranging my schedule and taking work home, but, as someone once sang, "I work all night, I work all day, to pay the bills I have to pay."

Sadly, it was ABBA.

7

Personal Spending

It's the "Don't Ask, Don't Tell" of Family Finances,
So Never, Ever Inform Me That "Waxing"
Doesn't Involve a Trip to the Car Wash

After five columns averaging more than $100 a week in savings, I was feeling pretty good. I was saving money, my readers liked the stories, and my $1,000 goal was solidly in sight.

My reverie ended when I saw the next category in my ten-week budget-cutting effort: personal spending. Would my wife and I be mired in a debate over the cost of the perfect hair colorist? Would I have to defend my purchases of collectible lug nuts and Love Potion No. 9 (aka gin)? Would I blurt out, "Pedicure? Who else looks at your feet?" thereby ensuring that my boy, Li'l Money, remained an only child?

Surprisingly, no.

Thanks to Robin Thompson at Budget Wise Consulting, we made "personal spending" the magical family budget category that ensures wedded and financial bliss, with no arguments about why I can't spend $30 on designer duct tape or accusations that Mrs. Funny Money frittered away our hard-earned cash at the nail salon. To eliminate petty squabbling over petty cash, we decided that family money would be divided into categories of "Yours," "Mine," and "Ours." Most income and expenses would be "ours," but each spouse would get money to spend as he or she saw fit.

Personal money is just that: personal. It's the "don't ask, don't tell" category of family finances. For a while, we each had separate checking accounts linked to the main family account, and as long as checks didn't bounce I didn't pay any attention, not even tracking or categorizing the purchases. I closed those accounts when the bank upped the minimum balance requirement and started hitting us with fees. But even then, personal spending, either on a credit card, by check, or with a debit card, wasn't anything I bothered tracking beyond classifying the transactions as "spending."

A check of this murky corner of our finances—don't ask, don't tell, remember?—found that Mrs. Funny Money and I each averaged slightly more than $52 a week in spending on snacks, skin cream, visits to Starbucks, and other sundries. Most of that showed up as cash withdrawals from ATMs, but debit card purchases gave me a notion of where my personal money was going—and there certainly seemed to be room to save.

My biggest personal outflow was lunch, which I should pack, not only for financial reasons but for health reasons as well, since I work a few blocks from Detroit's two greatest Coney Island restaurants. The ugly surprise was that I'd paid almost $10 a month in bank fees during the year, for ATM surcharges or when the account balance fell to the point of incurring a maintenance fee.

Robin had the answer: cash.

"When it comes to debit and credit cards, I call it 'magic money,'" Thompson told me. "You never see it as spending real money." Mostly, she told me, the problem isn't with our big, monthly must-pay bills, such as the mortgage, but in our less-structured discretionary spending. "These variable expenses get us into trouble because they're prone to impulse spending," she said. "We don't say, 'Wow! Let me make an extra car payment!'"

Robin suggested managing your cash using the old-fashioned envelope system mentioned in chapter 1. Later, we adopted the envelope system for most of our spending on entertainment. And to cut down on the hassle of having all kinds of checks waiting to get cashed by various baby-sitters (and having any forgotten ones trigger an overdraft), I use cash for those expenses, too.

Spending with cash doesn't just make what you're doing seem more real as compared to swiping a piece of plastic; it's also physically more uncomfortable. A study by Priya Raghubir, of the Stern School of Business at New York University, and Joydeep Srivastava, of the Robert H. Smith School of Business at the University of Maryland, College Park, found that "the more transparent the payment outflow, the greater the aversion to spending, or higher the 'pain of paying.'"[1]

In other words, sticking a crowbar into your wallet to drag out actual filthy linen greenbacks sends the message to your primitive, survival-oriented caveman brain, "This is real, dude, and who knows when we might really need these bills sometime in the future, when the pterodactyls attack." When you've got only a $20 and $10 bill left in your wallet and payday isn't until next week, that subtle message is what convinces you to forgo picking up that magazine in the lobby, candy bar in the vending machine, or *Jaws 3-D: The Director's Cut* at the drugstore.

Paying with any kind of credit card, though, prompts shoppers to spend 12 to 18 percent more. It doesn't matter what it is—a credit card, debit card, gift card or certificate, Monopoly money, IOU, excess children, or even trinkets and beads—using anything but hard currency unleashes your inner drunken sailor who will slap down his American Express Cadmium Card for the Blu-ray boxed collector's edition of *Hot Tub Time Machine*, *Little Fockers*, and *Paul Blart: Mall Cop*. And gimme two boxes of those microwave knishes, too.

ATM and bank fees

This was my biggest embarrassment of the entire ten-week series of columns: the fact that I was paying about $10 a month in fees to get back my own money at the automatic teller machine. I've railed against these outrageous fees for years and yet I still got nabbed by them.

You get hit by ATM fees when you withdraw cash from a machine that isn't owned by your bank. Actually, you get hit twice. First there's the convenience charge from the owner of whatever ATM you're using. In 2012, according to my buddies at Bankrate .com, you paid a record average of $2.50 to the owner of the ATM, a 4 percent increase from the previous year.[2] That fee is disclosed at the machine, usually with a sign on the outside (though that requirement was recently waived by the Obama administration bank lackeys) and with a warning statement on the screen during your transaction.

You'll find these fees in places where the ATM owner has you over a barrel, such as at an airport or the quaint, cash-only cider mill, as well as spots where you probably shouldn't be withdrawing cash: casinos, strip clubs, racetracks, and other locales where it's a safe bet that you're not making the healthiest financial decisions.

On top of that, your own bank (that's right, the place that already has your money and is duty bound to let you actually get at your dough once in a while) hits you with its own fee for going outside the bank's own ATM network. In 2012, that charge averaged $1.57, up 11 percent from 2011, according to Bankrate. If you think that total of $4.07 in average ATM fees for just one transaction is worth the "convenience," look at it this way: if you withdraw $40 for lunch or after-work drinks with the gang, you paid a 10 percent fee just to grab two $20 bills.

I will admit that some of that money goes to the networks that run the ATM system, so it's not all going to the banks. On the other hand, banks need to admit that having customers use *any* ATM is cheaper than what it costs them to operate brick-and-mortar branches or evening and weekend-drive-through windows, and much less than processing checks, and that if customers couldn't conveniently access their very own money in some manner, then those people wouldn't be bank customers for long. With most checking accounts that you access through an ATM, the bank isn't paying you a dime of interest (and at today's rates, that's about all you'd get even if they did). Instead, the bank is loaning your money out and is supposed to make its profits on the spread between the 00.00 percent interest that it pays you and what it charges on loans. (A quaint concept, I know.)

Instead, banks now make more than 20 percent of their income from sticking an ever-increasing number of ever-increasing fees to its own depositors. New federal banking rules and a crackdown by the Consumer Finance Protection Bureau limit some fees, but it's like squeezing a sausage—the bank fees just pop out somewhere else.

You can sidestep ATM fees with some shopping and planning. Online banks and some credit unions will give you a set number of free ATM transactions each month at any machine, or they rebate any ATM fees you pay. Credit unions also operate a fee-free network of machines, which you can find at:

- **Credit Union National Association**[3]
- **The CO-OP Network**[4]
- **Allpoint**[5]
- **STAR**[6]
- **MoneyPass**[7]
- **SUM**[8]

That's helpful, of course, but when you need cash you have to access one or more of these lists and hope there's a participating ATM close at hand, which isn't always possible. Once, at Disney World, I felt all smug that I'd looked up free ATMs at the park before we left home. Well, *you* try finding the stand-alone ATM of the Disney employee credit union that's situated at some faraway shuttle stop in one of the employee—I mean, "cast member"— parking lots. Perhaps you are more frugal than I, but I am not taking a bus ride out to Reedy Creek Improvement District Conservation Area 3-A just to save the cost of one ATM fee. Closer to home (as in, three blocks from my house), there's another free ATM listed at the electric utility repair center, which is a depot for big, hulking electric-line repair trucks behind barbed-wire-topped fences. I suppose I could access cash there during working hours, but driving around all the parked bucket trucks at 1 a.m. on Saturday night to get cash for the baby-sitter after a night out with Mrs. Funny Money probably won't work, and it might get me shot by a security guard.

I've found that it's easier to simply have a stash of cash. You don't have to carry your entire wad in your wallet or purse at all times though. Every payday, I withdraw our biweekly allotment for baby-sitters, entertainment, and spending cash for both me and Mrs. Funny Money. Cash for sitters and entertainment goes into two special envelopes (and no, I am not telling you where in the house). I distribute the spending cash to Mrs. Funny Money, who, for all I know, buries it in a Mason jar in a snowbank or stashes it in her snood. I stow mine in the sock drawer, where I can grab what I need when I'm choosing between the sweat socks and argyles. ("Hmmm, I need cash *and* it's time to do laundry.")

No ATM fees, no guessing how much spending cash is in your account versus money set aside for rent or the car payment. Using cash means I can't "forget" about an ATM withdrawal and take out too much cash, resulting in another sky-high bank fee, like a $35 ding for overdrawing our account. If I do run short, I can always hit an ATM, borrow from a friend, or write a check. But overall, going with the green lowers if not eliminates outright the habit of throwing my money away just to get my own money.

Freeing up cash

Shop around when choosing your bank, comparing fees, access to ATMs, minimum balance requirements, and overdraft charges. Free checking appears to be dwindling because laws now prevent banks from pigging out on your "free" account by sucking your balance dry with a plethora of hidden fees. You can still find free checking (try a credit union), but you may have to look around. Another way that you end up "paying" for free checking is by keeping a minimum balance in your account. That amount also has risen in recent years, to an average of $723.02, up 23 percent between 2010 and 2011. Keep less than that on deposit and you face a monthly fee just to keep your account open. That averaged $5.48 a month last year, up 25 percent from the year before. At some banks, the minimum balance requirement is $5,000.

The majority of banks, however, will waive monthly account fees if you have direct deposit or do business with the bank in some other way. Overall, 95 percent of checking accounts offer some way to avoid a monthly service charge. But that doesn't mean your bank will tell you about it if they up the fees or requirements on your account. More often, the bank changes the rules in the fine print of the account statement you don't read each month, then slaps you with the new fee later on. If you don't notice, or don't complain, you're losing each month. So take some time to find out if there are cheaper checking options for the asking at your own bank. The money market savings account at my bank upped the minimum balance and started dinging my account for monthly service fees until I switched to a straight savings account. The difference in the pathetic interest rate was, I recall, a quarter of a point.

If you travel a lot and don't like to carry wads of cash, look into one of the growing number of online banks that will let you access ATMs without a fee. With the use of mobile technology for deposits from a smartphone or a computer attached to a scanner, you may find that you can simply avoid the fee-for-all that comes with a conventional brick-and-mortar bank.

Making ends meet

If you're stretching every dollar until it whines like a toddler being forced to eat rutabaga, keep a close eye on your bank charges. Now, you may think that skipping cash and putting everything on a debit card is a good bet: it avoids ATM fees, you can track every $2 you spend on stamps, and you don't run up any credit card debt. But chances are your checking account balance gets down to a single digit a day or two before payday, and then one mistimed debit-card purchase, forgotten check, or overlooked automated debit can get you slapped with a bounced-check charge. That's often 35 bucks, and if you get hit with one, chances are you're likely to get hit with more. Often, the bank pays your transaction, based on your deposit history, through something called a "courtesy overdraft," which also carries the same hefty fee as bouncing a check.

The reason is that these kinds of fees are nearly pure, risk-free profit for the banks. They cover your transaction for a day or two, until your next paycheck is deposited, and collect a fee that, if it were a loan, would amount to a usurious rate of 900 percent. Banks sneaked courtesy overdraft coverage onto checking accounts for years, claiming it was a customer service, but, oddly, it was one they hid in the fine print of the contracts rather than touting on billboards. Also hidden: the much cheaper options for overdraft protection, such as linking your checking account to a line of credit, a credit card, or a savings account. New federal banking laws required banks to get up-front approval from customers for "courtesy" overdraft coverage, and banks went on a scare campaign to frighten customers into thinking they had no other options.

While bank customers at least have to opt in for such grotesquely expensive overdraft "protection" these days, another truly scummy bank trick remains legal, at least for now. This is the practice of "check ordering," in which banks clear your checks and debit transactions not by check number or in the order received. Instead, the banksters clear these items from the largest transaction to the smallest. What this does is create the greatest possible number of overdrafts—and fees for bankers.

If you have a $100 balance and have transactions for $10, $20, $40, and $80 hit the account on the same day, clearing the largest amount first results in three overdraft charges, even though only one item—the $80 check—puts you over your limit. The difference to the bank is that they get $105 for three overdrafts instead of just one already ridiculously inflated $35 fee. For years bankers told me to my face for years that it was "to better serve our customers," claiming customers wanted big-ticket items such as the mortgage and car payment cleared first. In fact, banks were so selfless in offering overdrafts, purely to humor us customers, that they never even charged us for the wheelbarrows needed to haul all that extra cash, an estimated total of $20 billion from debit and ATM overdrafts in 2009.

Yet every time I dared them to show me research proving that customers did, indeed, prefer having their biggest checks and debits cleared first, they couldn't. Banksters also couldn't dig up that mythical research when they got hauled into court over check ordering, which prompted Bank of America to settle one suit covering thirteen million accounts for $410 million after a 2½-year fight. Citibank and Wells Fargo changed their policy two years ago to end check ordering, and some larger banks also decline debit card transactions that will prompt overdrafts. But despite threats from regulators, the practice is still in use at many banks.

The bottom line is this: First, if anyone at a bank says something is being done "to serve you better," grab your wallet, your gas mask, and a pooper-scooper. Second, make sure you have the least expensive overdraft protection possible on your checking account. If you have cash stashed in an emergency account or savings account that isn't earning much, move it to a linked account to cover your overdrafts, since that's usually the cheapest option. Third, make sure you never have to use it. Keep a financial calendar (or even just a dated list) that shows when big transactions regularly hit your account, such as an automated student loan or mortgage payment, or regularly add those items to your check register or banking software. And thanks to online banking, you can check your balance any time of day or night, so do that once in a while, especially in the last few days before payday when things get tight. And don't forget to record paper checks; they aren't deducted from your online available balance until they've been cashed.

Another option is to set up account alerts to warn you by e-mail or text message if your balance falls below a certain limit. Smartphone users can see if their bank has a mobile app to check balances by phone or other mobile gizmo.

Yes, I know that a married couple with automated deposits and debits, two debit/ATM cards, and checkbooks are just naturally going to run into trouble tracking their account balances. It's easy to say, "Don't write checks when you don't have the money," but it's not so easy to do when modern technology is making that harder to track, and especially when thieving banksters are trying to rig your account so they can drain out more fees. This is why cash is a good option for all those $7 lunches and $3 lattes and $12 cab rides. Using cash insulates your checking account from having any of these little items become a big bounced check charge, as well as helps you keep your personal spending within your budgeted allotments.

Pinching pennies so hard that Lincoln gets a headache

Pay cash when you can and avoid ATM charges like they were the latest episode of *Girls*. If you're stuck, get cash back at a grocery or drugstore, but don't throw your money away on gum or a snack. Get something you know you need, like a can of diced tomatoes, a box of tissues, or, even better, the latest edition of your local newspaper. (Remember: newspaper ink absorbed by your hands helps prevent gum disease. Trust me; I was pre-med for two weeks.)

As much as possible, pay your big, regular expenses out of your checking account and make your variable, discretionary day-to-day purchases out of your weekly cash allotment. Of course, you're still going to need to buy some things with plastic, such as online purchases, plane tickets, and rental cars. Once again, while it seems like it might be the reasonable, financially responsible thing to do to use a debit card rather than a credit card, think again.

When times are hard, you want to avoid putting anything on your MasterCard or Visa, and you're probably regretting the things you've already charged and still are paying off. Naturally, you're keeping your credit line open for emergencies, such as a doctor's visit or new transmission. So you make your routine purchases, especially online, with a debit card. But that can be dangerous.

First, in the case of fraud, your credit card liability is limited to $50 by federal law. And if you have problems with a vendor you can dispute a credit card charge because there's a sort of firewall between you and your actual money—the credit card issuer who pays the vendor and, in turn, gets paid by you. With debit cards, a bank may voluntarily limit your liability for fraudulent charges, but that's at the bank's discretion, not your legal right. And if you have a dispute about an online item that the vendor says was shipped but you never received, your money is already gone. If you want it back, you'll likely be stuck trying to get the vendor to do the right thing.

Using a credit card instead of a debit card assumes you pay off those credit card charges instead of letting them mount up. The easiest strategy is to pay off new charges when you get the bill, or, if you're ordering online, just open up a new browser tab, go to online bill paying, and send a payment for the same amount to your credit card company right then and there. Even if you end up disputing the charge, your money is either credited back to you or applied to your card balance. If you can't qualify for a card or don't trust yourself with one, consider online options such as PayPal or giving money to a family member or friend and having them use their card to make the purchase.

A huge number of Americans avoid having bank accounts altogether because they fear losing cash to banks that grab their fees first, making a bank account more expensive than going to a check-cashing outlet or even a payday lender. According to the Federal Deposit Insurance Corporation, around nine million U.S. households don't have a traditional bank account, while twenty-one million Americans are lacking in traditional banking services. So you're not alone if you're bypassing a bank, but ultimately you are paying more for money orders, check cashing, prepaid debit cards, and more. If you've been scared off from banks, shop your local credit unions and let them know you want a simple checking account that won't trigger fees, so you can pay your bills and keep your money safe between cash withdrawals. Then skip or lock up the debit card so you can more easily track your balance.

Mrs. Funny Money and I stick to cash for most of our personal spending, and we use our bank's online bill-paying service. Gas and groceries go on an American Express card that gives us double reward miles for those purchases, which cuts our future vacation costs. That card is automatically paid each month, but AmEx sends an e-mail warning before the bill is due, so I can make sure it's covered. That just leaves checks for medical bills or the fertilizer service, plus the big recurring expenses such as the community docking fee, which we save for every month all year-round and are tracked in my calendar. All that's left is the odd debit-card transaction for things like grub treatments and spackle at (Why Did I Ever Buy a) Home Depot.

All of this minimizes the number of our monthly bank transactions, especially casual debit-card purchases that are too easy to forget, and consequently it limits the number of opportunities for our bank to pull one of its scummy, fee-inducing tricks.

Lunch

Okay, so ATM fees weren't the biggest chunk of my own personal spending, but they were the most maddening. I felt better about what I spent on lunch, which at least gave me something for my money, even if it was money I could have been saving by packing my own midday meal and snacks.

At the same time, paying for lunch most days ought to cause me as much embarrassment as blowing cash to get my own cash out of a machine in the wall. In my carefree, scufflin' bachelor days, my refrigerator looked like the set George Lucas used for the ice planet Hoth. It usually held nothing more than expired milk for my morning coffee and leftover Chinese takeout that looked like it was either very fresh broccoli or very old beef lo mein. But once I arrived at my happy domesticated "I do" days, the fridge was full. I simply wasn't organized or thoughtful enough to pack something before blowing out of the house in the morning. Worse, the leftovers were going to waste and unhealthy purchased lunches were going to waist—mine.

There's an interesting similarity between budgets and diets. Unlike other bad behaviors, you can't quit overspending and overeating by going cold turkey. (Mmmmm . . . cold turkey sandwiches!) If, for example, you've picked up the habit of snorting PCP to boost your mood, you can quit that altogether and know that life is going to improve. But there isn't any good way to "just say no" to calories and dollars that doesn't leave you starving, evicted, or both. The only answer is moderation and control, which is more of a challenge and, quite frankly, one that all of us will win some days and lose on others. As I write this on St. Patrick's Day, let me just say that when it comes to moderation and control, this is not looking like their day.

Freeing up cash

You'd be amazed at how little effort it takes to save a significant amount on lunch. A typical lunch in the cafeteria used to run me about $7 total, and often included the ever-tempting pizza the old *Detroit News* lunchroom turned out. Instead, I discovered I could get a week's worth of Weight Watchers microwave entrées, two bags of frozen mixed vegetables, and a half-dozen bottles of generic seltzer and cut my cost to about $4 a day. Sharing a newsroom coffeemaker with a half dozen other caffeine addicts brought my habit down from as much as $3.50 a day to the price of contributing a can of coffee once a month. The whole thing involved one stop at the grocery store a week, one Tupperware bowl, and remembering to take two minutes to grab the stuff in the morning. (Okay, three minutes, since I had to wash the Tupperware after forgetting to put it in the dishwasher.) I was saving up to $50 a month on coffee alone, and even more if I watched for sales.

Think that's not much? Let's say you have a credit card with an 18.9 percent interest rate and a $5,000 balance. Stick to the minimum payment each month and in about 11-and-a-half years you'll have paid back more than $8,100. Now add the $50 you're saving each month from bringing your own coffee to your minimum monthly payment and you'll pay that card balance off in four years and two months and save nearly $1,500 in interest. So buy your own coffee—just promise me you won't buy any French vanilla, which always tastes like I got my can of coffee grounds mixed up with Mrs. Funny Money's potpourri.

My daily savings on coffee and lunch added up to more than $60 a month in potential savings. (That's $15 a week times 4.3 weeks per month, because 52 weeks a year divided by 12 months = 4.3 weeks to each month. Got it?) I didn't completely stick to that schedule, and I forgot to pack lunch on some days or yielded to the convenience of cafeteria coffee over brewing a new pot. Of course, the frozen lunches and coffee were shifted to the grocery budget, so it wasn't all net savings, but I dealt with reducing our grocery spending later in my cost-cutting project. Even if I got sloppy and only brought my lunch from home two days a week, our personal spending was going to be a relatively easy category for finding savings. I'd just have to negotiate exactly how much we could cut with Mrs. Funny Money.

Making ends meet

Stretch things even further by planning ahead to use leftovers. If you're smart, you're shopping the groceries sales hard each week, stocking your pantry and freezer, and then planning your meals around those items you already have, plus picking up veggies and dairy. If you take the extra step to make your menu generate enough leftovers to provide lunch, or at least the basis of lunch, you can save even more and eat healthier.

If I'm making my aunt Frannie's ridiculously easy and wonderful chili, for example, I just double the recipe and I am set for lunch. I could eat that all week, quite honestly, although I haven't yet worked up to eggs and chili for breakfast. In the same way, an inexpensive bottom round roast yields sandwich meat and the leftover lettuce from a salad makes a good base for a lovely lunchtime antipasto.

This strategy involves one potential problem: certain other people in my household who don't happen to be my son will often bogart the leftovers, leaving a wide, hungry gap between my money-saving ideal and my stomach-growling reality. Either pack those leftovers for your own lunch right away, or, more responsibly, discuss who gets what when you plan the menu.

There will be days when it's not feasible to pack a lunch and other days when you're simply sick of brown-bagging it. Do what you can by bringing your lunch most days, and then splurge and go out to lunch with the gang every once in a while. Just make it a treat when you buy lunch and get something really good instead of blowing your money on a soggy vending-machine sandwich you could have made better and cheaper yourself.

Pinching pennies so hard that Lincoln gets a headache

Either get invited to a lot of business lunches or learn to love the brown bag. If you're financial squeakiness is caused by being out of work, that makes eating at home much easier, but also a lot more boring, isolating, and frustrating. Even if you do have a job, it's still limiting to chow down in front of your computer every day. You get bored, you get frustrated, and then you think, screw it, I'm never gonna get ahead, and next thing you know you're taking the whole department out for barbecue.

Let's be clear: nobody handles their money perfectly all the time, least of all me. I am not going to say I never got sick of the hassle of bringing lunch and eating the same thing. I occasionally said, "The hell with it," and ordered a toothsome sandwich from the deli and paid extra for delivery. It happens. But if you have a setback, shrug it off and don't consider that it will doom you to grinding penury for the rest of your life. Then think about what caused you to throw in the towel. Eating the same thing every day for a month? That'll do it. Agonizing over every possible expenditure and seeing a lifetime of doom if you don't do everything in the cheapest possible way? That'll really get you. You can't succeed at cutting your budget with a radical, unsustainable approach that leaves you no wiggle room or fun and no options except strict discipline 24/7. Taking that attitude is just as bad as a crash diet. You can keep it up for a week or two, but then you just give back all your progress.

To that end, see if you can't make lunchtime a way to bolster your progress and good intentions. I love this story shared on the budgeting site LearnVest.com by Erin Frank of New York City.[9] Frank works in publishing and credits a group "money lunch" with some coworkers for helping her knock out $35,000 in debt on a salary of just $30,000. After sharing her debt worries (mostly student loans but also credit card debt) with a few coworkers, they decided to brown-bag it together. Meeting regularly in a conference room at work, they shared money-saving strategies, created budgets, planned emergency savings accounts, and shared books and articles on various financial strategies.

That kind of arrangement with a few friends either from home or at work can create a good support network for the kind of long haul that's required to put your finances in order. It helps to have a few nonjudgmental buddies, not only so that you can see that you're not alone but also to help celebrate one another's progress. And instead of you all brown-bagging it, you can throw a potluck lunch or even organize a meal exchange. For example, in a group of four budget cutters, I make a batch of Aunt Frannie's chili and bring three extra servings in freezer bags to share. My three pals do the same with their mac and cheese, chicken and rice, or meatloaf and we all have three new meals for the price of just scaling up our home cooking.

People use support groups for everything from quitting crack to writing novels, and if those twin scourges can be conquered, there's no reason you can't do the same thing. And if you include me, you might just score a taste of Aunt Frannie's chili.

The Bottom Line

Goal: $1,000

Week 1—Transportation . . . $41.61
Week 2—Miscellaneous . . . $132.89
Week 3—Utilities . . . $139.39
Week 4—Kid Costs. . . $114.50
Week 5—Work Expenses . . . $90
Week 6—Personal Spending . . . $104
Total monthly savings . . . $622.39

Left to cut . . . $377.61

Beyond bank fees and lunch, who knows how you or anyone else will manage to cut back when it comes to personal discretionary spending? Lord knows that I don't want to know what Mrs. Funny Money spends her personal cash on and how she cut back, and I certainly would be embarrassed to have her know how stupidly I spent my cash in the past. But lunch is a good place to start cutting, and paying any kind of bank fee is just like burning your money, except less fun.

However you spend, you're likely to spend less on a cash diet. If you can't make that work, then you've probably set a spending limit that's unreasonably low, so go back and adjust. And when you do choose to spend, get the things that give you good value for your money and are important to you instead of casually throwing away $3 here and $5 there. If you give up the mediocre overpriced vending-machine snacks, you still can afford the good gin.

We had good luck using the envelope system. From now on, cash goes into one envelope for Mrs. Funny Money and another for me, along with cash for sitters and entertainment. When it's gone, we're done until the next payday. If we buy something online with a credit card, cash comes out of the appropriate envelope and gets deposited in the checking account to cover the charge.

After weighing all the options, Mrs. Funny Money and I agreed that we could each get by on personal spending of $40 a week instead of more than $52. If we saved a bunch on lunch, coffee, and bank fees, that freed up money for whatever else either of us wanted, as long as we stuck to the $40 weekly limit. That saved $104 a month, with nary a marital squabble, thanks to the very cooperative and understanding Mrs. Funny Money. Ideally, our new all-cash approach will allow us to find ways to trim without cutting out the things that are important to each of us.

"After all," said Mrs. Funny Money, batting her eyelashes, "new makeup and nice clothes make me feel romantic."

"Oh, sweetie," I said, handing her a martini, "that's what the gin is for."

$ 8

Entertainment

If You Must Resort to the Indignity of Using a
Coupon—and You Must—First Ask Yourself
WWBD? (What Would Bogie Do?)

After several weeks of saving more than $100, I was on a roll.
My family was saving money, readers liked the columns, and
I'd managed to keep raccoon off the menu. But things suddenly
turned discouraging when I turned my budget-cutting efforts to the
Funny Money family's entertainment expenses. I was supposed to
be cutting my spending there by $100 in Week 7, but all I wanted
to do was spend *more*. Adding it up, it didn't look like Mrs. Funny
Money and I were having much fun to cut in the first place.

Movies, concerts, and especially dining out are some of the first
things any personal finance expert will tell you to cut when things
get tight—and it makes sense. If you don't have an adequate emergency fund, are carrying credit card debt, or aren't saving for retirement, you need to cut back on the good times now to avoid bad
times later. And if you've seen your income drop or lost a job, it's
even more important.

But first, you need to be having some fun to cut back on.

As I scanned our list of entertainment spending, a few things were missing: limos, fine restaurants, concerts, plays, nightclubs, and—more importantly—baby-sitters. In their place was the local sports pub, diner, gym, and, seventh on the list, McDonald's. All exceedingly family friendly, and all places we regularly took my boy. But entertaining Li'l Money left his parents with li'l fun.

Now don't get me wrong: there's no fun like family fun. Visiting the pool at the gym put such a smile on my boy's face that I'd play in an ABBA cover band for tips before I'd cut the gym membership from the budget. And a family movie or breakfast out at the start of the weekend was likewise worthwhile. But out of $366 a month in entertainment spending, just one-sixth went to date nights for Mr. and Mrs. Funny Money—and that was in a good month. Instead of whispering sweet nothings into my money honey's ear over crepes suzette, I was shouting above the din at the Burger King playground.

Look: if every meal out comes with a toy, it's time to rethink how the fun funds are spent. It was clearly time for us not only to cut out casual drive-bys at the drive-through but also to reallocate our entertainment expenses to movies released by a studio other than Disney. Our move to Michigan came only a few years after Li'l Money arrived, and his mother and I hadn't completely made the mental switch from being a childless couple with two incomes and nights and weekends off to being the kinds of people who spend an entire weekend sleeping, eating, shopping, and cleaning without ever changing out of our sweatpants.

Mrs. Funny Money's schedule of working Wednesday, Friday, and Sunday nights didn't help either. On these evenings I'd make dinner and leave a plate out for her. Then, as she slept in the next morning, I'd check to see if she had eaten. The whole thing was about as romantic as leaving cookies out for Santa Claus.

Cutting our spending on entertainment while at the same time finding more ways to get the planets that rule our schedules and budget to align for more date nights was going to be a challenge. But looking over what our finances said about the state of our romantic life led me to one simple conclusion: when it came to dining out, it was time to give chicken fingers the finger.

Dining out

Since we are parents of a grade-schooler, most of our entertainment spending revolves around movies and eating out. Family fun was mostly Cub Scout activities for the boy, family get-togethers in the park next to the lake, and the odd trip to a museum, science center, or anything with a train. Vacations are a separate category where the expense is covered by additional savings or freelance income, so I don't make it part of the budget. Instead, it's an "extra" that needs to be covered with "extra" money, not the regular household income from paychecks.

Economizing on movies was easy. We switched to earlier weekend show times that were cheaper and signed up for a discount card that rewarded us with free popcorn or beverages after so many films. Mrs. Funny Money and I also trimmed our movie viewing to take advantage of our cable offerings or library DVDs. Our criterion became whether a film was "big-screen worthy" or would lose too much in translation from a movie theater to the TV screen. That means we go out to see *Lincoln* and *Life of Pi* but wait for *Bachelorette* to show up on cable (and then, I hope, find something else to do). Since the gym that we joined for pool privileges offers a parents' night out deal once a month, we can score cheap babysitting ($20) and a movie at reasonable rates.

That just left eating out as the big nut to crack.

Freeing up cash

There's an old saying that, whatever you want in life, you can get it cheap, easy, or good, but you can't have all three. That's certainly true with eating out. We were getting a lot of drive-through or pick-up food that certainly was easy but probably not good (or at least healthy). And, once I added up all the quick hits at $8 here and $3 there, I saw that it wasn't all that cheap, either.

The reason was our overall lack of preparation when it came to shopping and menu planning, and our failure to coordinate Li'l Money's dinner with his parents' habit of not eating their own evening meal until at least 9 p.m. If there was nothing in the fridge or freezer and nobody felt like running to the grocery store, the default was to pick up something from a casual restaurant or fast-food joint. Instead of getting something fun for our money, we were just plugging holes in the weekly menu.

This really had more to do with the grocery category that came later in my budget-cutting experiment, but once again it demonstrates how letting one budget category get out of control can slop over to disrupt others. In the same way that planning the week's cooking, meals, and grocery shopping cuts down on personal spending for lunch during the week, it also reins in the urge to throw away your entertainment money by grabbing ready-made grub just because you're irritable and hungry and you don't know what to cook.

Once again, this is where switching your discretionary spending to cash can help out. As with the personal spending described in the last chapter, we decided to switch our entertainment spending to a cash-only system. The allotment for our entertainment expenses goes into a special envelope after each payday, and that's it until the next check arrives. If we forget to grab cash and put a meal out on a debit or credit card, the cash gets removed later and deposited to cover the bill. When the money's gone, you either have to find some other cash (if I've worked at home for a day and saved on the after-school babysitting, for example, then some cash is freed up) or you go without.

This not only sets a limit on spending but it also dampens the urge to spend spontaneously without thinking. If Li'l Money was agitating in the back seat for chicken from the drive-through and I hadn't picked up a few bucks from the entertainment envelope before we left home, I faced three choices. I either swipe the debit card and remember to move enough cash to cover the expense to the bank deposit envelope, use my own personal spending cash, or convince the boy to wait for some healthier air-popped popcorn and juice when we got home.

Remembering to transfer cash was just enough hassle that I'd get home and forget, which continued the problem of overspending on fast food. Using my own cash, I found, motivated me to more often remember to reimburse myself, and, if I didn't, it forced me to cut back on my own spending, leaving the cash in the entertainment envelope untouched. The best strategy, of course, was to substitute something the kid likes at home and, I hope, teach him a valuable lesson in deferring gratification, or at least give him plenty of material to chew over with his future therapist.

I'll add that seeing the cash pile up in the entertainment envelope turned out to be the biggest motivator of all. I was slightly thrilled when, after getting cash from a paycheck, I'd go to refresh the entertainment envelope and find cash leftover from the previous two weeks. I'd stealthily count up the leftover bills, compare it to the cost of a night out and a sitter, and see how much more we needed. That gap was enough to make sure that Mrs. Funny Money and I remembered to set aside coupons from the newspaper ad inserts for the casual restaurants we'd hit with Li'l Money, and to recall which ones let kids eat free on which days.

The system worked well enough that I also switched the baby-sitting payments to cash. First, it made it easier to balance the checking account, instead of having multiple checks for $25 or $36 floating around to a half dozen different sitters, who might cash them only sporadically. More important, it motivated me to get home on time or even early so that the baby-sitting envelope would accumulate its own buildup of cash that could be reallocated to a date night. I even picked up some colorful expanding cardboard envelopes and broke out the label maker. I resisted the urge to start clipping out pictures of fancy dinners and dancing couples clad in ball gowns and tuxedos to decoupage the envelopes, lest the whole thing start to look like some thirteen-year-old girl's Pinterest board. Although I might still cave and tape on a color photo of a juicy rib eye and a well-chilled martini.

Clearly, if paying with cash causes a physical reaction akin to pain as we saw in chapter 7, saving cash must have an equal and opposite effect, just like in physics, right? Well, according to a University of Minnesota study, the soothing power of greenbacks isn't just psychological. Actually handling cash can ease the sting of physical pain, emotional discomfort, or personal slights. The study had subjects count out paper or money, then dip their hands into scalding water. The subjects who handled the money reported feeling less pain.[1]

Which gives me an idea. Now when Li'l Money starts up his whining when we bypass McDonald's, I know just what do. While he quiets downs as soon as he gets a snack at home, the same doesn't always apply to Daddy's jangled nerves and headache. Now I can just rub the extra entertainment cash against my temples.

Making ends meet

C'mere. Over here. Listen closely. Guys, I am going to tell you how to drive a woman crazy in fewer than ten words, and I do not mean, "Not now, honey, the game is on." Ladies, I must warn you that this all-powerful technique is the kind of potent aphrodisiac that will cause your husband to view you as a combination of Rachael Ray and Jessica Rabbit in yoga pants.

Whatever your gender, I am trusting that you will use the power of what I am about to reveal only for good and not for evil, such as getting out of your turn to chaperone the Cub Scout sleep-away.

Here's how it works: You enter the room and pry her away from Facebook (in the case of a woman) or prod him off the couch (man). Looking him or her intensely in the eye, you reach into your pocket/wallet/bodice/chest waders and withdraw an intriguing slip of paper. Wordlessly, you unfold it and present it to your mate. Maintaining eye contact, and in a low, sultry voice, speak these words: "Weeknight date night. With. A. Coupon."

Trust me, you're gonna need either smelling salts or a cigarette.

Whether it's a Groupon bought online, a coupon clipped from the newspaper (remember: prevents gum disease!), or a two-for-one deal from a your credit card company, nothing perks up the week of a hard-core married couple like the promise of a midweek meal that's eaten not off the coffee table but from an actual linen tablecloth at a restaurant where the maître d' sniffs, "Booster seat, monsieur? I do not think I am acquainted with ze term."

When money's tight it's really tempting to zero out your spending on any kind of entertainment, especially eating out. But I simply believe this is unsustainable. If you don't get a little crazy, you're gonna go more than a little crazy. It's better to plan and find the kind of deal that makes you both go "Squeee!" at the thought of rewarding yourself for your budget discipline. Locking down every dime means that eventually something snaps and, when you finally track down your wife somewhere in Vegas, you find her eating caviar off the abs of a Chippendales dancer.

Trust me. Meal planning, shopping for bargains at the grocery store, and learning to love every part of the chicken—except the McNugget!—will be much easier to bear if you get out for a good crab cake once in a while. Otherwise, you become one very crabby cake yourself.

It's easy to sign up for online deal sites such as Groupon, which will e-mail you specials. Don't grab every one that comes your way, since that defeats the money-saving aspect of this project, and you're likely to end up buying deals that expire before you can claim them. At *The Detroit News*, we have our own similar offer, Deal Chicken, which presents offers from our advertisers, so check to see if your local paper offers it or something similar. Other sites include Living-Social, Amazon Local, and Travelzoo. Look around on the Web and test out one or two at a time to keep from being overwhelmed. Set up your e-mail so that the offers go to one folder so you can review them without having them clog up your inbox, causing you to miss that important e-mail about your forthcoming Genius Grant (I'm still waiting, MacArthur Foundation. . . .).

Naturally, your weekly newspaper flyers and coupon mailings should be reviewed instead of trashed or thrown in the fireplace, and check Valpak.com, the online site for the outfit that mails out those big packages of coupons. Another very good resource is the ads in the newspaper's weekend entertainment sections, which usually appear on Friday or Thursday, and the local alternative paper (look between the ads for DUI lawyers). But often the best sources for discounts are companies with which you already do business.

Some of the best dining deals I've ever gotten came via my American Express card. During slow times of the year, restaurants would occasionally send out discount cards that knocked as much as $50 off a meal at an upscale steak house, for instance. I can't predict when these things will show up, but, along with reviewing the offers stuffed in my monthly statement, it makes going through the junk mail more like a scavenger hunt, and if you don't, you'll regret it. During a busy period last fall I let the promotional mailings pile up unopened, and when I went through the stack I found two expired promotions for a free entrée at a very upscale joint. I furtively ran them through the shredder before Mrs. Funny Money could find out about the missed opportunity.

Other sources include getting on the mailing (or e-mail) lists of your favorite restaurants, or the ones you *want* to be your favorite restaurants, and just keeping an eye out when you're there. Restaurants tend to promote themselves the most to their repeat customers, so, for instance, the most likely spot to see that the Harbor House down the street offers a Saturday-night deal with two entrées for $30 is by stopping by the Harbor House once in a while.

Once you land a dining deal, don't undo the frugality by going hog-wild on drinks, appetizers, and dessert. Apply your coupon or deal, know what you can afford, and split an appetizer or dessert if you must. A glass of wine apiece or a carafe of the house stuff will be fine with dinner. Plus, you don't want to linger too long and run up the baby-sitter bill. But, if you've saved enough to go whole hog and it's in your budget, then shoot the moon and tell 'em to bring on the cheese course.

I'll share this strategy that my parents employed when our family first moved to the suburbs and their fun funds were scarce. My mom set aside a jar for all their quarters. If she had two bits left after grocery shopping or my dad had a few in his pocket at the end of the day, into the jar they went (this was the early 1970s, so maybe use dollar bills today). After enough money had piled up, it was date night for Mom and Dad. This could take a while, so to stretch their bucks and increase the frequency, they skipped cocktails at the restaurant. Now, for an Irish-Catholic couple, you might think this would defeat the whole point of the thing, but Mom was resource-ful. Once Dad was all freshened up and she had on her dress and fancy shoes, they left us boys in the basement game room, broke out the booze and mixed nuts, and adjourned to the living room, which in that era, was off-limits to the kids (the velvet ropes my mom hung in the doorway were a subtle reminder). There they'd hold their own discount happy hour before heading to the restaurant.

If you're using a coupon, be warned that this can be an issue for some people—notably men. The reason is that fussing with scraps of paper seems wimpy, not manly. Try to imagine Bogart using a coupon. Or Paul Newman. John Wayne might have used a coupon, but only to roll a cigarette one-handed on horseback while firing a six-shooter. And don't even think about Sean Connery's James Bond using one:

> **Bond:** A dry martini.
> **Barman:** Oui, monsieur.
> **Bond:** Three measures of Gordon's, one of vodka, half a measure of Kina Lillet. Shake it until it's ice cold, then add a large thin slice of lemon peel. Got it?
> **Barman:** Oui, monsieur.
> **Bond:** Err, I say, I have a 30-percent-off Groupon for any mixed drink. Can I still use that?

Not suave. You can just hear Pussy Galore snickering.

Coupons simply go against a guy's inner big spender, who, in-stead of unfolding a clipping for $1 off, screams, "Throw down a $50 and tell 'em to keep the change!" Nonetheless, real men can use coupons—we just get someone else to push the paper, preferably a child, a woman, or a Frenchman. Here's how Bogie would handle it at the end of *Casablanca*.

Captain Renault: It might be a good idea for you to disappear from Casablanca for a while.

Rick: I could use a trip. But it doesn't make any difference about our bet. You still owe me ten thousand francs.

Captain Renault: How about a buy-one, get-one-free coupon for appetizers at Bennigan's!

Rick: Louie, I think this is the beginning of a beautiful friendship.

So remember: look for deals and clip those coupons, and the cost of a date night won't amount to a hill of beans in this crazy world.

Pinching pennies so hard that Lincoln gets a headache

You may be broke, but you still gotta have some fun, and cheap fun is the best kind of all. Dining out is going to be tricky, and rare when your finances put you up against the wall, but it is possible.

First, throw out your dinner plans and substitute lunch, which is often less expensive. You may also be able to park the kids at an activity and skip the cost of a sitter. Another bonus is that it's easier to get reservations and linger at your table than it is during the Saturday-night dinner rush. You're also more likely to skip expensive drinks or limit yourself to a single glass of wine at lunch. No wine steward rolls out the port cart at noontime. And if you do need to imbibe, see whether it's a better deal to bring your own bottle of wine and pay the corkage fee at better restaurants. This isn't an option in my home state of Michigan, because our state liquor control board is run by money-grubbing Puritans. But if you live in a more enlightened locale, call ahead and ask the restaurant what they'll charge to handle your bottle. Just please don't bring anything in a box, and, if you do, don't you dare mention that this was my idea.

Another way to keep your dining bill low is to eat in the off-season. Summer is a slow time for many restaurants, and it can be a big time for bargains. For a few years of my misspent youth, I was the editor overseeing restaurant reviews in Palm Beach. Once the 90-degree days and infestations of love bugs drove the snowbirds back north in May, the finer restaurants trotted out their summer menus. These featured four-star selections at nearly terrestrial prices, often in prix fixe deals that offered an appetizer, salad, entrée, and dessert for one price. The practice is pretty common, so you should find it being offered during whatever the off-season is where you live, too. Check the Friday entertainment section in your newspaper (gum disease!) and watch the online specials, or check with the restaurants themselves. Another potential bargain spot is restaurants in hotels and resorts. They have to remain open, but with a smaller number of guests during the slack season, they often run specials to fill the dining room with locals.

Another tactic comes from my former running buddy in New York City, The Big Man from Brooklyn, who's now happily ensconced in Florida (where, unlike most city transplants, he doesn't insist on driving 32 mph in the passing line of the turnpike with his blinker permanently on). The Big Man has become a mystery shopper, which means he gets paid to try out a variety of goods and services, then files a detailed report to aid the company in improving its products and customer service. At first, The Big Man focused on services that he usually paid for, such as oil changes, but he can also score assignments to check out movie theaters, and he's added some impressively upscale restaurants to his roster. It's extra work, and most times it still costs him a few bucks in the end, but it's the perfect way to get some entertainment for nearly free.

"It certainly works if you've got three hours and can type and pay attention to details," The Big Man says. "You're not saving money if it's not stuff you have to do. I don't have to stay in a hotel in Fort Lauderdale or go to Outback Steakhouse, but I do have to get my oil changed, so if I mystery-shop a Jiffy Lube, that's 40 bucks in my pocket. But I can get dressed up, take my mom out to a fancy steak house, and get a $200 meal for three hours' worth of work."

To do that, The Big Man has signed up with a mystery shopping service and e-mails to volunteer for specific assignments, which are posted each month. He then has a variety of detailed observations he has to report, including specific aspects of his customer experience, such as how long he waited to be greeted, did he notice a manager on hand, and even how his menu was presented at the table. He may have to follow a specific procedure to make the reservation, bring a companion, order a drink at the bar first, note the condition of the restrooms, and order a set number of dishes. And he has to submit all this within about twelve to twenty-four hours after visiting the restaurant.

The Big Man found his mystery shopping company by searching the Web, but watch out for frauds. Any place that requires you to pay money up front should automatically be considered suspect, and definitely check with the Better Business Bureau and search online for complaints before putting up any of your own cash and hoping to be reimbursed. A good place to start is at the Web site of the Mystery Shopping Providers Association North America,[2] the trade association representing the "customer experience metrics industry." The Web site includes a good guide for those who want to become shoppers, and it offers a certification program ($15 or $75), which may or may not help you land more work but is designed, the association says, to train shoppers on what to expect and to offer tips on how to work efficiently. The site also has a full rundown on avoiding scams and notes that real mystery shopping firms don't ask you to pay them or offer to pay you in advance, which is a scam to stick you with a bad check. You can check legitimate mystery shopping firms at the association's site and contact them directly.

The one drawback to mystery shopping is that . . . it's a mystery. That means you're not telling the staff and eating for free, but instead paying up front and waiting to be reimbursed once you file your report. You'll need to either float the cash in advance or carry the charge on your credit card. If you use plastic, be disciplined enough to deposit your entire payment to cover the charges. Don't use the money for other purposes while your card balance swells, since adding debt defeats the idea of saving money.

In many cases, The Big Man notes, what you're paid won't cover the entire cost of your purchase, but in that event, he's warned in advance. He also checks online to see menu prices. A dinner for two at a high-end steak house, for example, runs about $220 with tax, tip, and valet, but he only gets $200 for the review. At other times he has mystery-shopped a Checkers drive-through, a much easier assignment. "That was the cost of a No. 3 combo that I didn't have to spend, and I didn't have to have peanut butter for lunch on Tuesday." A recent assignment to mystery-shop a movie theater offered $7 and covered two tickets and up to $6 for a beverage.

Overall, The Big Man says, "The companies know exactly what they want, and if you're willing to do it and wait for your money, you can go have a very nice dinner for nearly free."

Other dining deals include frequent-diner cards, which offer items such as a free entrée or meal for every ten paid meals. The Entertainment.com coupon book (based right in here in Metro Detroit, I'll note), which is often sold during fund-raisers by schools and other nonprofit groups, can be another source of savings. A coupon for car rentals paid for the price of the book in our case, and there were enough offerings from restaurants we know we like to make it worth the effort to dine on specific days or from limited menus.

The Bottom Line

Goal: $1,000

Week 1—Transportation . . . $41.61

Week 2—Miscellaneous . . . $132.89

Week 3—Utilities . . . $139.39

Week 4—Kid Costs . . . $114.50

Week 5—Work Expenses . . . $90

Week 6—Personal Spending . . . $104

Week 7—Entertainment . . . $108

Total monthly savings . . . $730.39

Left to cut . . . $ 269.61

With our entertainment expenses averaging $85 a week, the bulk of it was for dining out, with $66 a month going to the gym so that Li'l Money could play in the pool. In the last month there had been exactly one grown-ups-only outing, for a whopping $55—not even as much as the gym membership. A few months earlier, it was all fast-food and family dining, with nary a date night in the bunch.

It was clearly not going to hurt anybody in our household (and, in fact, it would make us healthier) to cut back on this category altogether and to direct more of what was left to restaurants that don't feature sporks. Trimming $25 a week produced monthly savings of about $108 (remember: 52 weeks a year divided by 12 months = 4.3 weeks to each month). The entertainment category was a good candidate for a cash-only envelope spending approach, which not only discourages overly casual spending on casual dining but also encourages stockpiling cash for a big night instead of a Big Mac.

The quest to save can become all about spending less, but you also need to weigh how much you get for your money. In our case, it wasn't enough. And since we couldn't add a couple hundred bucks a month for visits to restaurants that don't hand out crayons when they seat you, we not only needed to spend less, but we also needed to think more about where we did that spending.

I decided we should celebrate our new approach to fun at the Funny Money house and planned a sophisticated night of grown-up amusement. It would be just the kind of adults-only bonding that holds a marriage together.

"Honey," I said to Mrs. Funny Money, "let's go out and have some fun tonight."

"You bet!" she replied, heading for the door. "But if you get home before I do, leave the porch light on."

9

Life Insurance

A Big Monthly Bill Is the Answer to My Nightly
Prayer, "And If I Die Before I Wake, I Pray
My Wife a Huge Wad of Cash Takes"

After fixing up our fun fund, I had to deal with a real downer: life insurance. Yes, it was one of our top ten spending categories, and the monthly premiums were nearly as much as our entertainment budget. Which prompts the question: What does it say about us that Mrs. Funny Money and I spend nearly as much just trying to live a little as we do on an investment that'll pay off only if one of us dies?

It's no shock that entertainment and meals out claim a couple of hundred dollars a month from our budget. But it was quite surprising—and seemed deeply unfair—to find that amount nearly matched by our $299 monthly life insurance premiums. And, as with any china I chip or spills I neglect to wipe up, I blame my boy, Li'l Money.

During the B.C. (before child) era, Mrs. Funny Money and I carried life insurance that covered little more than paying off the mortgage. That coverage came as a benefit from our two full-time jobs, which provided about a year's worth of income to the bereft

137

surviving spouse. Beyond that, both of us made good salaries that would allow either one of us to carry on alone, using any extra money from life insurance payouts to overcome our grief, in the arms of either Harrison Ford or the ladies of the Victoria's Secret catalog.

After we moved to Detroit, I became the family's primary bread-winner, and my untimely death would call for a payout that retired all our debts and would support my wife and son at least until the boy is through college. And should Mrs. Funny Money prematurely shuffle off this mortal coil, I'd need a good-size wad to cover every-thing she does, from acting as chauffeur and cook to teacher and nanny.

These kinds of shifting family situations are why insurance cov-erage should be reviewed every two years according to Ronald Os-tezan Jr. of Insurance Partners Agency of America in Troy, Michigan.

In some cases, he said, policyholders neglect to change their beneficiaries and end up leaving a fat insurance check to an ex-spouse. In other cases, coverage needs to be changed, family mem-bers have been added or passed on, or whole life and universal life policies that include investment elements didn't perform well be-cause of changing interest rates.

Here's the thing: any kind of insurance is a bet. A bet against you getting on the plane with the three bad engines, the drunk pilot, and the flight attendant who just broke up with her fiancé. A bet against a wrong-way driver who thinks your exit ramp is his freeway entrance back to Passaic. A bet against what you remember from shop class thirty years ago versus the label on the back of your stereo amp that says "NO USER-SERVICEABLE COMPONENTS INSIDE!"

But this is a bet that you really, really don't want to win, and, when you lose, you should count yourself lucky. It's like all those people who worry about some weird worst-case scenario (bears, vol-canoes, or, worse, bears that throw you into a volcano) and figure that worrying about those things means they won't happen. Car insurance means an alien spaceship won't land on my wife's Mercury. Homeowner's insurance means my house wasn't built over a zombie moose burial ground. Disability insurance means the collator on the copy machine at work won't seize my festive Halloween tie and drag my noggin through the stapler attachment. When you write that check or see that automated debit for the premium, you are more than free to resent it, just as long as you remember that losing a bet against losing your own life is a great big win.

How much insurance do you need to leave behind for your loved ones? If you can afford it, you should try to cover:

- Paying off all household debts, including the mortgage.
- A year's worth of living expenses for your loved ones, so they can figure out just what to do now that you're gone.
- Enough money to support children and other minor dependents through college.
- And, if your spouse doesn't work outside the home, enough money to support him or her through to retirement, or at least make up for the loss of your income.

That can add up to a pretty big tab. The cheapest approach to covering it all is term insurance. As the name suggests, it covers you for a fixed term. Then the coverage expires, and all your premium payments are lost forever. Which, again, should be a reason to celebrate.

In my case, I aim to pay everything off and support Mrs. Funny Money and Li'l Money through the kid's college graduation, after which the Widow Funny Money can start claiming our retirement benefits. I figure that a cool $1 million invested conservatively can produce enough income to do the trick (remember, initial insurance payouts aren't taxed as income).

It's trickier with Mrs. Funny Money, especially when she wasn't working outside the home. Her lack of income made it hard to get as much coverage as I felt we needed. You can't really put a price on the value of a caring, nurturing mom, but that doesn't mean people don't try. The folks at Insure.com estimated the 2012 value of a mom at $60,182 (down about 2 percent from 2011, so step it up, ladies), but I think the insurance guys vastly underestimate the street value of a real-world mother.[1]

According to the "Mom Salary Wizard" at Salary.com,[2] a full-time mother of one school-aged child in my home of Oakland County, Michigan, puts in ninety-five hours a week as everything from chauffeur to janitor to logistics analyst, at a median value of $116,000 a year, or $141,000 on the high end. (For stay-at-home dads, the "wizard" calculates fifty-three hours a week with a median value of $64,000 and a high of $81,000, but I think this figure ignores the amount of effort it takes to call your wife at work seventeen times a day for guidance in operating the Crock-Pot.)

The price tag on a working mom is less—a median of about $69,000 and a high of $85,000—but that's counting only the value of her efforts at home. To get a full picture of the insurance needs, add the net income a working mother also produces. Either way, if one parent disappears, you need to cover not only whatever financial contributions he or she was making to the family but also the value of everything else he or she contributes, from laundry and yard work to cooking and sump pump maintenance.

If Mrs. Funny Money were to, shall we say, involuntarily enter the fertilizing business, that would leave me with seven more years to tend to Li'l Money before the boy heads off to college, meaning I'd need an inflation-adjusted payout of $999,000 at the median level and $1.2 million on the high end. Which definitely proves that I am not exaggerating when I tell her, "Honey, you look like a million bucks!"

As swell as having all the right insurance can be, there is a lot of useless stuff out there. For example, you may have burial insurance on your kids, something that somehow gets sold around the time babies are born. You may have cancer insurance or some odd breed of short-term disability coverage marketed by a duck. Most of this specialized stuff isn't a good buy and may not be necessary. Cheap term insurance can cover any final expenses. If you have a child with major health issues, juvenile life insurance might be a smart move when they're young, but sort that out with a good agent. In most cases you are better off saving the premiums on these very specific types of policies and putting the money toward good comprehensive life, disability, and health insurance, as well as your emergency savings.

Freeing up cash

There are two different types of life insurance: term and whole life. Term, as we discussed earlier, is a bet between you and the insurance company that you won't expire before your coverage does. Remember, if you lose the bet (you don't die), you win because, hey, you didn't die.

A drawback is that once the term expires, the premiums you've paid are gone for good. Buying a whole life policy—also called "permanent insurance"—puts your premium to work as an investment as well as providing a payout if tragedy strikes. This added benefit doesn't come for free, which is why whole life insurance is more expensive. Whole life can also carry higher commissions and fees and can offer a much more limited range of investment options than the thousands of mutual funds you can access through a regular old Individual Retirement Account.

At the most basic level, financial planners say that it's usually simpler and cheaper to keep your insurance and investing separate. Insurance is about managing risk ("What if a piano falls on me?"), while investing is about growing your money ("I think shares of Steinway Inc. are about to take off!"). Personally, I think it's generally best to pursue each goal separately by purchasing term insurance to cover your needs and investing separately in a well-diversified portfolio of low-cost mutual or exchange-traded funds. This advice, however, won't work for everyone, because whole life insurance can be useful in specific situations, such as insuring children with major health issues who may have trouble buying their own policies later in life. You can also take loans against a whole life policy, skip premium payments at times, and take advantage of all kinds of other options.

Whole life insurance also is a very nifty and highly flexible estate-planning tool. If you're one of those rare individuals who regularly max out contributions to your 401(k) or similar workplace retirement savings plan as well as your IRA options (both regular and Roth), a whole life policy can offer big tax advantages for sheltering investments from Uncle Sam. Which is why asking any question of a good personal finance advisor is like the old joke about Ronald Reagan's underwear. When the Gipper is asked, "Boxers or briefs?" he responds, "Depends." Figuring out which insurance approach is best for you depends on all kinds of very individual factors about you, your family and business, and your financial goals. The right kind of whole life policy might be the perfect tool to meet your needs, but so might term insurance. What's the right answer? Depends.

What this all means is that whatever kind of insurance you have, you need to make sure it fits your needs and fits them now. So, if you haven't gotten help in making an overall insurance assessment in several years (or ever), get yourself an appointment with a couple of well-established independent insurance agents and start gathering advice. Even if you don't need to make a major change in your coverage, it still pays to shop around and compare prices, which vary dramatically. If you decide to stick with whole life, for example, look for a low-load or no-load policy with lower expenses, which can be hard to find but are usually offered through fee-only financial planners.

I know that insurance agents sometimes get a bad rap. There's an old saying, "Insurance doesn't get purchased, it gets sold," which is as much about our unwillingness to recognize our mortality as it is about the aggressive tactics of some insurance agents. I've met people who were sold stunningly overpriced and inappropriate variable life annuities after attending a "free" steak-dinner "investment seminar" at a local hotel. At the height of the financial downturn, as stocks and most investments were taking savage beatings, many investors tangled up their real insurance needs with their worries about their investments and wrapped them up in various insurance products. If this applies to you, you need to get some expert help to look objectively at your insurance requirements, which will be different than your investment goals.

On the other hand, I've also seen our family insurance agent do a flatly wonderful job at protecting and managing the nest egg my late father left for my mom using a strategy that included some very good fixed annuities. Like auto mechanics and waitresses, there are good insurance agents—even great ones—and bad ones. You can find a guide to evaluating agents at Insure.com.[3] If you find an agent who's well versed in all aspects of financial planning, he or she can gauge how your insurance fits into your overall plan. But if you are looking for a more comprehensive approach to your finances than just making sure your spouse can pay the bills and get the kids through college after you catch the big dirt nap, try an independent, fee-only certified financial planner. You can find a list of those folks on the Web site of the Certified Financial Planner Board of Standards.[4]

Making ends meet

If you're just squeaking by, term insurance will likely be your best bet, but, again, talk to a couple of agents before you make a decision. You can also compare prices and find a lot of good information online. The better you understand this stuff, the better shopper you'll be.

Before you start comparing prices, stop and reevaluate your needs. In my case, I bought my last big life insurance policy when Li'l Money was five years old and the stock market was climbing to a record high. The number of years of family expenses the policy would need to cover is smaller now, but, thanks to the recession, so is the nest egg I expected Mrs. Funny Money to see from our retirement accounts. So some recalculating may be in order for our family, and it probably is for yours, too.

If your needs have changed and you think you'll want coverage for several more decades so that a more expensive whole life policy makes sense—or that you'll have to move that way in the future—consider starting with cheaper term insurance but getting a policy that you can convert to permanent life insurance.

The rule of thumb with insurance is that the younger you are when you buy it, the lower your premium will be. Remember how insurance is a bet? Well, if you buy life insurance at ninety years old, there's a good chance the insurance company won't collect many months of premiums before you die, and your costs reflect that.

(The same applies to long-term care insurance, which covers the costs of illness and old age. Experts recommend that you start shopping for that coverage in your early fifties, so I guess that should be added to my to-do list for this year, and I'll have to do some more budget cutting elsewhere to offset the cost. I may finally have to start using those AARP discounts. Damn.)

Once you've compared prices and updated your coverage, there are a few other things you can do to bring down your premium. One is to look at the price breaks available as you move through levels of coverage. Life insurance tends to get priced at so much per $1,000 of coverage, but that rate often goes down as you hit certain levels. So, if the per-$1,000 rate drops above, say, $250,000, it can be cheaper to get $260,000 of coverage than $225,000. Another option is to start with a low-level whole life policy and adding term insurance to it through what's known as a rider, which adds on specific benefits.

One item to nix is the accidental death (or double indemnity) rider, which pays extra if you get flattened with the aforementioned piano instead of slowly succumbing to beriberi. Now, stop and think about this: How will the financial needs of your family really change because of the manner in which you die? Well, if you succumb to some dread, lingering disease, you might leave behind quite a pile of hospital bills. But a double indemnity rider only pays off if you die in an accident. What's the big extra cost there? Flying your corpse back from that weekend in Vegas? (Where, in all likelihood, your last words were "Hey, honey! Watch this!")

The only way I can see that an accidental death rider might be a good buy is if you work in a very dangerous job and can't afford to buy all the regular life insurance coverage your family needs. (By the way, according to the U.S. Labor Department, the most dangerous job in the United States is taxi driver and not, as you probably imagined, fire fighter, lion tamer, or pediatric dentist.) For most of us, however, double indemnity coverage is nothing more than a way for an insurance agent to grab a few more bucks. If you do buy double indemnity coverage, don't tell your spouse or you'll never enjoy another Barbara Stanwyck movie again.

In general, look at what any type of rider is supposed to cover and see whether you're better off just buying more coverage, getting a separate policy, or self-insuring by putting what you'd spend on the premium into your emergency fund. A rider that guarantees you can increase your coverage later with no medical checkup can be skipped if you just buy the extra coverage now instead of waiting. A long-term care rider, for example, can be complicated, and it might be better simply to shop for a separate long-term care policy.

Life insurance coverage that specifically pays off your mortgage or sends your kid to college is simply too narrow to make good financial sense. Instead, use that money to prepay your mortgage (if it makes sense), save to a college fund, or simply increase your overall life insurance to cover those costs. The first reason for doing so is that the most likely scenario is that you're *not* going to die anytime soon, but you still need to pay the mortgage and get Junior and Missy off to study art history and bong hits at State U. The second reason is that your spouse's financial situation might mean that he or she uses your life insurance payout for something other than paying the mortgage, such as now, when the stock market is rising and mortgage rates are at near-record lows. Or maybe your kid wins a scholarship or goes to electrician's school.

That said, even the most complicated and specific rider does have a good reason for existing, even if it doesn't apply to most people. If your family medical history includes big, scary diseases that you have a good reason to worry about, the option to add guaranteed life coverage with no medical checkup can be a way to lock in a low premium before you display any symptoms. Likewise, an accelerated death benefit, which pays a certain percentage of the face value of your policy if you become terminally ill, might make sense for someone who is at high risk for one of those conditions. So, again, it's going to depend. The point is to get educated, shop around, shop around some more, know what you're buying, and make a decision that works for you. But if you just start checking off boxes on a policy at a Web site or on the other side of a salesperson's desk, you're probably overpaying for your coverage.

Pinching pennies so hard that Lincoln gets a headache

If you have a full-time job, start by checking your employee benefits. You may already have some free or very cheap life insurance coverage of up to one year of your salary, and many companies will allow you to buy additional coverage, usually up to double or triple your annual earnings. Coverage up to $50,000 is tax-free to you, and payouts to your survivors under that amount won't be taxed, either. But anything over that amount, including additional premiums you pay, will be paid with after-tax dollars. Since that will lower your take-home pay, shop around and see whether it's cheaper to buy your own coverage, which has the additional benefit that you won't lose it if you lose your job. On the other hand, make sure that whatever coverage you're automatically getting from your employer is factored into your overall insurance needs. If you decide it'll take $300,000 to cover your family and you're already getting $50,000 at work, you can lower your outside coverage.

What else is free when it comes to lowering your life insurance tab? We've already talked about knocking out excessive coverage and unneeded riders, determining an appropriate level of coverage, and comparison shopping. But there's one more option: get healthier. When it comes to that whole betting scenario, insurance companies long ago figured out that people who are overweight, have high cholesterol, smoke, and have other lifestyle risks are more likely to die while they're covered. Naturally, the insurance companies charge more for those conditions.

If you've had some serious health issues, you may have gone out and purchased a "guaranteed issue" life insurance policy, which requires no medical screening and only that you answer some basic medical questions. If you had trouble finding a regular policy, this may have seemed like your only option. A better choice may be to shop for an insurer that specializes in covering people with your specific condition. These companies usually have a better, more nuanced approach to pricing that reflects how you're managing a chronic condition, such as diabetes, that can lower your premiums. The conditions that get hit with the highest premiums are heart disease, cancer, diabetes, obesity, and asthma or other pulmonary conditions. If you have trouble finding affordable coverage, ask your broker to check with carriers that specialize in "impaired risk" insurance.

The next step is to get healthier. Smokers can pay twice the rate on some policies as nonsmokers, and that includes users of e-cigarettes, cigars, pipes, weed, and hookahs. I don't know if the group of smokers includes the kind of guy who puts a hard sear on his steaks over the charcoal grill, but give 'em time. And, yes, smokeless tobacco counts, too. When it comes to lowering your costs, however, you have to quit, not lie about quitting, or, if you die of smoking-related disease, your insurance may not pay off. Losing weight, lowering your cholesterol or blood pressure, and keeping chronic conditions in check by following medical advice all can help you lower your risk profile and your premium. Even if you've already got a policy, request a review if you've improved your health. Insure .com has some very helpful tips on what you should and shouldn't do before an insurance physical, such as limiting your caffeine intake for forty-eight hours.[5] You'll be grumpy, but you'll pay less.

Similarly, if you used to have a dangerous occupation that resulted in a higher life insurance premium—say, as sky-diving instructor who moonlighted as a bomb-disposal technician—renegotiate your coverage now that you're an actuary working in a nice, safe office.

Another free option for trimming your insurance costs, if you can swing it, is to switch from monthly to annual or semiannual payments, which will lower your cost by 10 to 20 percent. This can be quite a chunk of cash for an old fart like me with a high-value policy, but for a healthy young person looking for $250,000 of coverage, the annual premium could be less than $200. Even if you only save $20 a year this way, that's $20 that can go for something else.

Disability insurance

When most people think about insurance, it's life insurance, but the truth is that although we're all going to die, most of us won't do it while the kids are in grade school. According to the Social Security Administration and the National Vital Statistics System, you are much more likely to be injured or too sick to work than to die before retirement. You are more than twenty times more likely to die after hitting retirement age than before you see your forty-fourth birthday. On the other hand, more than one out of every four workers in their twenties today will become disabled at some point before they're old enough to retire. If you're disabled for more than ninety days, you are likely to be disabled for up to two years.

What this means is that if you want to focus on insurance, worry more about disability than death, especially if you're young. In some cases, you get short- and long-term disability coverage through your workplace, which typically replaces 50 to 60 percent of your income after ninety days for long-term disabilities. That coverage is cheap, about $30 a month, even if you have to pay for it yourself, according to the Consumer Federation of America. Unfortunately, the Bureau of Labor Statistics finds that 68 percent of private-sector workers lack disability coverage.

Buying your own coverage is one answer. In some cases, you can continue to pay for a workplace policy at the same low group rate if you move on. One benefit of buying your own, however, is that you'll always have it, and the payments won't be taxed as income, while payments from a pretax workplace benefit are taxed. To produce $3,000 of monthly income for me, the premium on an independent short-term disability policy would be about $68 a month. The payments would be tax-free, kick in after ninety days, and last for up to two years. I could pay more and get coverage that starts in thirty days. Balance whatever workplace benefits you get (vacation and sick time can cover a couple of weeks in most cases) with your savings to see what you'd need to scrape by. For longer-term coverage, I could add a policy that runs for ten years or up to age sixty-seven. The cost depends on your age, health, and gender, how long you want benefits to last, and how much time you can afford to wait until the policy starts sending you checks.

Another important distinction between workplace disability policies and those you buy on your own is that, under federal law, with a workplace policy you can't sue for additional damages if your claim is denied. This means those insurers aren't worried about getting hit with damages if they turn down your claim, which, according to some experts, makes them pickier about approving payments.

Another disability benefit comes via Social Security Disability Insurance, but that takes a while to process, perhaps as much as six months, and, with plenty of government-mandated red tape, there's no guarantee you'll actually collect. The average benefit in 2012 was about $1,100, according to the Social Security Administration, covering conditions expected to last for at least a year or—bummer alert—cause your death. Most private disability policies will require you to apply for SSDI benefits and deduct any money you receive from their payments to you. Once you qualify for Social Security disability benefits you can apply for Medicare, but there's a two-year waiting period. Until then, you'll also have to cover your own health insurance costs, so plan for that, too.

Finally, when shopping for disability insurance, pay close attention to how the policy defines "disability." Is it when you're unable to do your job, any similar job, or any job that pays the same as your old salary? In addition, long-term conditions may be capped at a maximum payout for certain conditions, such as mental illness. Also ask what the policy means by income; it usually doesn't include bonuses and commissions. Since long-term benefits can last for a lifetime, look for a cost-of-living adjustment so that your payouts won't be eroded by inflation. Make sure you understand how much you'll collect, when you can collect—and when you can't.

For more information on disability coverage, check out the Web sites of the Council for Disability Awareness[6] and the Social Security Administration,[7] or download a guide from USA.gov.[8]

Freeing up cash

Chances are you've been focused on life insurance rather than disability, so first assess your needs. As you shop around for your life insurance policies, look at the options to add private disability insurance. The savings you find on life insurance may offset what you'll pay for disability coverage. And remember to see if any of your current policies allow the option to add disability as a rider or other feature and whether that might be cheaper than buying a separate disability policy.

If you decide you've been spending too much on life insurance and want to shift that money to disability coverage, don't cancel your life insurance policy until you've gotten a replacement. You may find that a new policy is more expensive or harder to find. If you haven't had a physical in a while, an insurance exam might turn up something that would raise your rate or disqualify you for coverage.

Making ends meet

If you've got a workplace policy, check to find out if you can continue that coverage if you leave your job. If that's the case, you can continue to get by with what you've got at work, then pay to take it with you if you leave. If your premium is included as a benefit or partly subsidized by your employer, you'll have to pick up that expense, but because of the group rates provided to employers, it'll probably be less expensive than buying your own individual policy.

If you've opted in for additional coverage, you can consider temporarily cutting back to save money for a while. In many cases an employer might offer limited disability payments or coverage—say, 50 percent of your pay—but you can pick up the cost of increasing the coverage to 60 percent or more. If you did that years ago, you can opt for a lower amount of coverage now, then return to the higher level when you've got more breathing room in your budget. Check with your benefits rep in human resources, or, as we old-timers call it, "personnel."

Pinching pennies so hard that Lincoln gets a headache

If you've got workplace coverage, that's your best bet. Beyond that, you'll either need to dig up the money to pay for a basic policy to cover you if you can't work or build up your savings and support network. And that goes without saying if you're scraping by and not working, since you've got no income to insure.

Problems like getting too sick or hurt to work show the wisdom of the old hippie aphorism, "Life is like a junk sandwich, man. The more bread you have, the less junk you swallow." That is the philosophy behind establishing an emergency fund; even if you only sock away a couple hundred dollars, it can make a big difference.

Start by setting aside even the smallest amount—as little as $10 a week—automatically in a savings account. I suggest 2 percent of each paycheck, or $2 out of every $100 you take home. Put it in an interest-bearing account with a low minimum balance, such as an online money market savings account. This adds the benefit that you can't instantly drain your emergency fund when you suddenly decide to redefine "emergency" as "drunken road trip to Daytona Beach."

Your rainy-day fund won't grow much, but at least it's there. At 2 percent, you'll save the equivalent of one week's pay every year. Since the minimum goal most planners recommend is enough money to cover three months of living expenses, you can see that regularly saving a small amount is a slow way to go. On the other hand, I can think of many, many times in my scufflin' Washington Heights days in New York where even that small amount of money would have made a big, big difference in solving a problem. If your disability stretches on for years, even the biggest emergency fund won't cover all of your expenses, but it can cover you if you lose six weeks of work because of a badly broken leg, and it can prevent the kind of short-term financial problems that can spiral into a real crisis.

So, try to up that savings rate on a regular basis, maybe adding another 1 or 2 percent every few months. But you can make a bigger, faster gain by making a solemn promise to yourself that you'll put at least half of any kind of financial windfall into your emergency fund. That means a tax refund doesn't equal a blowout weekend getaway, but maybe a nice dinner out and a big chunk added to the emergency fund. If you get paid weekly, there are four five-paycheck months in the year (two if you get paid semimonthly), so you should dedicate as much as you can of those "extra" checks to your rainy-day account.

While the three-month rule is a good one (and since the recession I have met many good financial experts who recommend eight

months of emergency savings), don't let that discourage you. Set a
short-term goal—$500 or $1,000—and work toward that in whatever way you can, even if it only involves cashing in your returnable
Budweiser cans. Remember, you don't need to cover three months
of earnings, just three months of living expenses, which, if you do
all the trimming we're discussing here in this very handy and entertaining book you so wisely purchased (or at least borrowed from the
library), is less than your total monthly income.

Personally, the Funny Money family has never accumulated
more than slightly over two months of living expenses in our emergency fund. But, since we replenished it whenever possible from
windfalls, it saw us through a nearly ten-year period when we went
from two full-time incomes to one or one-and-a-half, at best. But I
can't discount luck and the fact that the prime breadwinner always
managed to stay employed, so I'm still working to boost that balance
well beyond the three-month minimum. "It's better to be lucky than
smart," goes the saying, but if you're smart enough to have some
savings, your luck will stretch a whole lot further.

If you can afford it, having an emergency fund and disability
insurance is your best approach, because you'll have more options
and more of a financial cushion if you do become disabled. So, if
things improve, leave your emergency fund intact and go shopping
for disability coverage. But, if you don't have any income, you're
going to have to self-insure with your own savings.

If you become disabled, you may get some additional protection
from Social Security Disability Insurance, but that can be hard to
collect. Consider that in 2012, 2.8 million people applied for disability benefits, but only 980,000 claims were approved, a rate of
35 percent. An injury or disability may also be covered by workers
compensation in your state, but that won't apply if your injury happens off the job, which is far more common. Still, you should apply
for these and any other assistance programs for which you qualify

if you're sick or injured and unable to work. Just remember that beyond your own savings, your own insurance, and the charity of family and friends, there aren't any guarantees.

Wills, medical directives, and more

I know that this thrilling discussion of death, dismemberment, and disability—and the minutiae of the varying approaches to insuring it all—has you perched on the edge of your seat, meaning that you can't wait to finish this chapter, leap up, and go do just about anything else, such as paint a barn. But I would be irresponsible if I didn't run down a list of other steps you should take to insure your family finances in case of a major emergency, such as having an up-to-date will. It's said that you're not really dead until someone says your name for the last time on Earth. Well, die without a will and you are going to be damned near immortal, as the people stuck with sorting out your affairs in the unending circle of probate mutter your name often and darkly.

So, let's make sure that you have all of the following.

An up-to-date will: Single folks with no kids can get by with cheap or free forms from Web sites or software, but if you have lots of assets or children to provide for, you'll need a lawyer. For a good overview, check out Nolo.com (they also sell software to help you make your own will, which I've never tried). One way to keep your costs down is to use an online or software product as a tool to create your own will, then have an attorney check it over. If you're strapped, look for legal clinics or call a law school to see if they offer help.

A durable power of attorney: This provides for someone to make decisions in case you are temporarily incapacitated (or, as we call it at my house, "Saturday morning"). Generally this is your spouse, but you should also designate someone as your secondary "agent" if your first choice is unavailable or unwilling. That way, someone can make decisions if both you and your spouse lapse into short comas after eating from the same tray of dollar-store sushi.

You can find forms online, often from your state bar association or attorney general's office. Your financial institutions may have their own forms, and using those will make it easier to deal with them specifically. Again, free forms, Web sites, and software are a good start, but unless the paperwork comes from an official source, such as your state bar, it would be best to have it looked over or prepared by an attorney. You folks with legal insurance should get a free will or a discounted one every few years, so ask about that.

Health care power of attorney: This allows someone to make health care decisions for you if you are incapacitated. You can find these online (I found a good one at Right to Life of Michigan, for example),[9] but you need to keep this up-to-date, as health care laws change. If you have a very old one that was completed before health care privacy laws were instituted, it won't be accepted. That means you could actually put someone in the position of being charged with making your health care decisions while leaving them unauthorized to actually discuss your medical problems with your doctors. So get the new forms, or hope they guess right.

List of accounts and passwords: Collect all of your insurance accounts and contact numbers, your log-in and passwords for your online savings accounts, and so on. This has been called your "death dossier," and the folks at *The Wall Street Journal* have a nifty graphic called "The 25 Documents You Need Before You Die," which outlines just about everything you need to leave behind for those you leave behind.[10] Note: not having these doesn't mean you won't die, just that the hapless schmuck sorting out four file cabinets of your bank statements going back to the '70s will wish he could.

Beneficiaries: Make sure your retirement accounts, bank accounts, life insurance, and other policies all designate an up-to-date beneficiary who gets your dough when you go. At this very moment, there are thousands of ex-wives in this country who'll get all of their first husbands' insurance and 401(k) payouts if the guy kicks off tomorrow, all because he's never updated a simple little form. Updating your beneficiaries avoids expensive probate hassles and allows your grieving spouse to pay the bills instead of being evicted while he or she is wrangling with lawyers. (Also, wouldn't *Wrangling with Lawyers* make a great reality show? I'm envisioning attorneys in three-piece suits trying to outrun rodeo cowboys on horseback as grieving widows and orphans cheer. TV producers, call me!) Don't, however, name minor children as beneficiaries, which will create all kinds of probate trouble. Instead, get your will done and establish a trust for the kids, and the trust will become the beneficiary.

Update it all: Got married? Got divorced? Got any new kids? (Hint: check the sofa cushions.) Any big life change means it's time to check and update all of the above—your will, your insurance, the works. You might think this isn't a problem, but believe me, it is. As an example, Mrs. Funny Money had a *very* nice employee stock option plan at her old job, which built up a tidy sum over more than two decades. Had something untimely happened to her, there was paperwork naming me (and, by extension, the nearest Porsche dealer) as the beneficiary.

But although she hasn't died, her company did, and her stock benefit was automatically transferred to a newly created Individual Retirement Account after the bankruptcy. That new IRA had no beneficiary named until she recently got a letter saying, in effect, "Hey, we don't see a beneficiary here, and, should something dire occur, surely a nice gal like you must have a special someone to receive all this dough."

That was last month, but the money was transferred to the IRA six months ago, and during that time I wouldn't have been able to get a penny of it without a lot of hassle and cost. Fortunately, she's been eating her vegetables, so it wasn't an issue, which is maybe the nicest thing I ever will say about Brussels sprouts.

The Bottom Line

Goal: $1,000

Week 1—Transportation . . . $41.61
Week 2—Miscellaneous . . . $132.89
Week 3—Utilities . . . $139.39
Week 4—Kid Costs . . . $114.50
Week 5—Work Expenses . . . $90
Week 6—Personal Spending . . . $104
Week 7—Entertainment . . . $108
Week 8—Life Insurance . . . $64.40
Total monthly savings . . . $794.79

Left to cut . . . $205.21

Because I'd been a pretty careful shopper on insurance, I didn't find much savings in this category. I already paid for increased disability insurance at work, but that was cheap. Beyond that, my only other insurance was the bargain-basement rate on a $100,000 policy that I described in chapter 3. We had bought limited coverage for Mrs. Funny Money after moving to Michigan, and that was at a good rate since the policy was only a few years old.

The only way I could save was to shop around and combine my separate life insurance policies. Our family insurance guru, Ron Ostezan, priced new policies and estimated I'd save an average of $64.40 a month. That was well shy of the $100 in savings I was hoping for, but with the extra cost cutting from previous weeks, I still came close to the $800 goal for the eight weeks of my budget-cutting experiment, missing it by a mere $5.21. That left $205.21 still to cut from the two remaining budget categories.

I also discovered that Mrs. Funny Money was completely clueless about our life insurance coverage. She had tuned out everything I'd ever said on the subject, putting it on the list of topics to safely ignore, a list that includes "specs for the new table saw," "Pinewood Derby speed tips," and "every word my husband has ever uttered about fly-fishing."

I was taken aback at first, then reassured that she trusted me to make sure she and Li'l Money were adequately provided for in the event of my untimely demise and during what I'm sure would be a minimum five-year period of mourning.

"So you're really not worried about what you'd get if I died?" I asked.

Mrs. Funny Money surveyed the bleak Michigan winter landscape out our window. "Oh, I know exactly what I'd get," my wife said evenly. "A condo in Miami."

$ 10

Groceries

Or Why Your Author Suspects There's a Darn
Good Reason That You Don't See TV Ads
Proclaiming, "Mutton! It's What's for Dinner!"

M y whole reason for tackling The $1,000 Challenge was food.
When my *Detroit News* colleague, the shy, teetotaling
wallflower Charlie LeDuff, turned in a column where he described
a guy selling raccoon roasts, it got me thinking. Had it come to this?
Were people really showing up at the door of Glemie Dean Beasley,
a licensed Detroit raccoon hunter, furrier, and meat salesman, and
heading home with raccoon as an entrée?

The idea of eating raccoon was oddly intriguing, and it appealed
to the gritty urban scavenger gene that I think all Detroiters inherit
at birth. I tried to figure out exactly how I'd get Mrs. Funny Money
to go for a raccoon roast. Beasley barbecues his with a vinegar brine
and spices and says it tastes like mutton. I didn't think I could sell
her on that, since I don't see a lot of TV ads touting, "Mutton! It's
what's for dinner!" Maybe, I thought, I could dress it up in a fancy
mustard sauce and shroud it in a French phrase, like *cuisse de raton
laveur à la Normande et son écrasée de pommes de terre*. Or perhaps,
with Detroit being so close to the Canadian border, I could whip

up a French-Canadian inspired ragout, perhaps a *fricassée de chat sauvage*.

Alas, *non*. I couldn't think of any scenario where I ended the meal saying, "And guess what, honey? It's raccoon!" that didn't involve Mrs. Funny Money rushing first to the bathroom and then to divorce court.

Fortunately, I was able to abandon the idea of serving up fricassee of furry bandit thanks to another language I was learning to speak. Rather than French, I took up the study of "couponish." And the most useful word of all that I learned was "BOGO." (It stands for "Buy One, Get One Free," as they drop the F. It's not to be confused with YOLO—"You Only Live Once" which is the phrase youngsters use to excuse anything excessive or stupid these days. Such as chowing down on raccoon.)

Thanks to BOGO, as soon as I finish this paragraph I will sit down not to raccoon but to a toothsome bottom round roast that cost me exactly $0.00 per pound. The other roast that I bought to get this one free was $5.99 a pound on sale, so I ended up paying $3 a pound for both. Mr. Beasley's $12 raccoon roast serves four, while the bottom roast serves two, which means the math works out against raccoon, at $3 a serving, and in favor of the round roast at $1.50 per plate. The only way raccoon would be a better deal were if the critter knocked on my back door, doffed his pelt, and climbed right into the oven on his own.

My introduction to lingo of supermarket savings came thanks to Teri Gault, founder of the Grocery Game, an online guide for combining coupons and store sales to produce sizable savings. Gault's company surveys ten thousand items at major grocery chains each week to find which are at their lowest price and matches them up with available coupons for additional savings.

Her strategy relies on the fact that most items in the supermarket go on sale at some point every twelve weeks, down to their rock-bottom cost. Adding the coupons from newspaper inserts and signing up for mailers from the grocery store cuts the cost even more, occasionally even making some items free. When Teri took me shopping on a visit to Detroit, we scored two gallons of free milk by purchasing several boxes of cereal with a special coupon. By pulling out the coupons and stocking up whenever grits, Gatorade, or Glad bags were at their lowest prices, she explained, I could likely cut my already trim household grocery tab of $532 a month in half. The trick, she said, is to plan meals around the cheap stuff you've stocked up on instead of making a weekly menu first and then shopping to fill it in.

Doing the latter "puts people in a vicious cycle of paying full price for 70 to 80 percent of what they buy," Gault said. Surveys of Grocery Game users, who pay $5 for the weekly guide, find the savings for a family of four averages $512 a month, she added. Partly that's because she looks at all the savings on food that come with strategic grocery shopping that replaces fast food and any meals that are eaten out simply because there's nothing in the house or no dinner has been planned.

The result is that you can enjoy some significant savings without eating like a pauper. The technique is pretty easy to pick up, and even if you don't use Teri's system, you can just start keeping an eye out for specials and sales. The bottom round roast, for example, I spied while popping into the store to pick up something for my mom. I recognized it as a previous good deal and snapped it up. Sure enough, when I checked, there it was on the weekly Grocery Game list marked in blue, Teri's code for "invest," indicating something you should stock up on—if you'll eat it. This tends to fit in with my own philosophy of building systematic savings into the things and services you buy most frequently.

Taking a further look at the current list, I see red and yellow bell peppers on sale for $1 apiece. These are staples in our house, either for grilling with other vegetables in the summer, or, in winter, sautéed with onions, turkey meatballs, and the mouthwatering tomato sauce Mrs. Funny Money cans with our friend Cynthia. I had already purchased frozen ground turkey at a rock-bottom price at Costco a few months before and converted the first few pounds into a batch of spiced meatballs, which we split into two-serving batches in separate freezer bags. Now I can grab $2 worth of peppers and sauté them with the onions, olive oil, and garlic already at home. While that's cooking I thaw the meatballs, throw half a jar of sauce in the pan, add the meatballs, and there's a really good, really cheap main dish. I could add pasta to stretch it out (Teri lists Mueller's Whole Grain at $1.17 this week, not a rock-bottom price, but good if you need it), but I usually just grab a manager's special on a bagged salad mix and skip the carbs.

Another recent item on sale was whole cooked lobster, $5 each for some pretty small ones, 12 to 14 ounces. Generally I prefer a 2½-pounder with lemon and drawn butter, thank you, but for a Valentine's weekend dinner, I grabbed three of the little guys, picked out the meat, and made a recipe of lobster stew with a pastry lid. That didn't involve anything other than grabbing a leek and a lemon and using the staples at home (butter, spices), half-and-half (already on hand for Mrs. Funny Money's morning coffee), and some leftover puff pastry stuck in the back of freezer. I added a salad and one of the fresh half-baguettes that go on sale at the local gourmet market after 4 p.m. for half price. At $20 (plus white wine, already on hand), it made for a slightly pricey dinner for two at home, but for a special weekend meal it was a heckuva lot cheaper than getting a sitter and going out.

The idea is that, whatever approach you use to shopping for food, if you stock your pantry and freezer with stuff you like when it's cheap, you can plan your meals around what's on hand and what's cheap or fresh this week at the store, the farmers' market, or even your own garden. And you don't have to concentrate on packaged, processed stuff or eat things you don't like just because they're on sale this week. The downside is that it takes some planning, but you don't need to shop every week other than to pick up dairy and vegetables. On those occasions, I will check the blue items on Teri's list and try to grab a few. Sometimes I don't even need to do that, since I now recognize the real bargains as they come around again.

I am much more lax about using coupons, mostly because I have wasted a lot of time on grocery coupons in the past. Most coupons I found were for items we didn't use, and it turned out that even with 50 cents off, name-brand items often cost more than store brands. With the Grocery Game, I only need to keep two types of coupons, those that come in the mail and those from the Sunday paper. I don't even clip them, but I just file them by date in a manila folder and pull them out when they're called for. I usually forget, though, and just concentrate on the big sale items.

Freeing up cash

Once upon a time, when the newlywed Mr. and Mrs. Funny Money had two incomes and hadn't sentenced ourselves to death by children, we made out a sort of menu, went shopping, and added whatever suited our fancy. Then we paid the bill because whatever it cost was what food costs, right? Hahahaha! It was a simpler time, and by that I mean we were idiots.

If you're not putting any kind of thought into how you shop for groceries and plan your meals, your grocery bill is going to be the easiest place to score some big savings in your family budget. You don't have to spend hours collecting coupons, run from store to store, or convert your garage into a giant walk-in pantry, either.

Start, as always, with the items you use the most and look for ways to consistently find them cheaper.

One big payoff comes from nongrocery items, such as paper goods, sandwich bags, dishwasher soap, and so forth. I've found the best balance between price and quality at warehouse stores such as Costco, and in most cases the store brand works fine. Otherwise, at your grocery store, start with the cheapest stuff you can find and, if it's not good enough, work up to the least expensive acceptable brand. I did this with paper towels, which are a major food group at our house, at least when I cook. I'd buy a cheap roll, take it home, and, when I unwrapped it, put the wrapper inside the cardboard tube. On the next shopping trip, I took the wrapper with me. If the towels had been lousy, I moved up to the next price level. If the towels worked fine, then I kept getting that brand.

The next step is switching to store brands and generics for packaged food. I have found no canned item, for example, where the store brand isn't just as good as a nationally advertised brand. Also, most canned goods at our house, such as the diced tomatoes that go into Aunt Frannie's chili, are used in recipes where spices and other ingredients are going to drown out any subtle difference between the national brand and a generic. In fact, except in rare cases (maybe a favorite pasta sauce, balsamic vinegar, or olive oil), I don't think you'll taste any difference when it comes to most things that are canned, packaged, or bottled. The only two things on earth where I insist on a specific brand are mayonnaise (Hellmann's, and don't you dare bring me any of that Miracle Whip stuff!) and Inglehoffer creamy horseradish. Since we maybe buy a jar of each twice a year, we're not talking about big bucks here.

That'll get you some savings right there, with no effort other than scanning the shelf to look for cheaper brands. When it comes to things like produce, dairy, and meat, you'll need to check out the weekly store specials, manager's specials, and fliers to see what's on sale. Or you can use a tracking service, such as Grocery Game. Also, keep an eye out for price stickers and in-store promotions indicating that the store may be clearing out slow sellers. When you spy these items on sale, stock up. Once you become conscious of prices and consistently shop for the same items in the same stores, you'll recognize that, say, 99 cents a pound for frozen turkey breast (especially the kind your wife likes) is a deal and that you should grab a couple for the freezer.

Another easy way to save on groceries is to see if your store has a loyalty program. Here in Michigan, grocery stores are big on everyday low prices—but only for customers with a store loyalty card. Then you get the specials, the ten-for-$1 promotions, and so on. The store managers don't do this out of the goodness of their hearts, of course, but to keep you coming back and to tailor the inventory and specials to what they see you buying every time you swipe that loyalty card. But, every so often, we get a mailing out of the blue with customized coupons for things we tend to buy. That package also includes one or two customer appreciation coupons that offer $5 off any $50 grocery purchase or $2 off any $10 (excluding milk) from the dairy department. That, my friends, is free money, and you didn't even have to print it yourself and face federal charges.

Yes, I said it—coupons. Okay, I know what you're thinking: Brian, did you just say the "C word"? You've watched those TV specials and there is no way you are going to become one of those wacky coupon fanatics who fill the spare bedroom with bargain cat food to trade with their neighbors for oatmeal.

I remember the case of "Coupon Connie" from the early 1990s in south Florida. Connie became nationally known for being able to use coupons to the point that she'd walk out of a grocery store with an entire cart of free items, with the store refunding cash on top of it all. Connie was known to rummage through trash bins for box tops and product codes to redeem, but eventually she wound up being inadvertently snagged into a criminal operation that exchanged counterfeit coupons by mail. A federal judge gave Connie twenty-seven months in prison, even though he felt she hadn't actually set out to break the law. (At the time I tried to convince my newspaper to use the headline "Coupon Connie Gets Clipped," but the editors ignored me. But here it is, twenty-two years later, in my book, so put *that* in your ninety-day performance improvement plan, suckers!)

So, yes, I can see how it's easy to get carried away with coupons, so we'll hold off on that a bit. In the meantime, let's talk about saving on groceries by doing more with what you get, whether it's with a coupon or not. For the Funny Money family, real savings comes from cooking stuff once and using it for several meals. That bargain turkey breast I mentioned? First it got roasted for a nice Saturday family sit-down dinner. (Yes, we actually got two working parents and their child home at the same time, sitting down at the same table, and, most amazing of all, forgoing chicken nuggets and all eating the same thing. I have alerted *The Guinness Book of World Records*.)

The remaining turkey went for sandwiches, a reheated leftover dinner, and a last sandwich or two with canned soup when I worked late, and then the remaining carcass got stuffed into a slow cooker along with a bouquet of spices, onions, and whatever was getting ready turn in the vegetable bin. Mrs. Funny Money left that bubbling down for a day or so, and we had a big batch of lovely homemade turkey soup to eat and freeze. The original turkey cost less than $10 and yielded at least six meals. Ben Franklin wasn't kidding when he called it a noble bird.

The same trick works with 2 pounds of flank steak on sale for $3.99 a pound. Two 12-ounce steaks get marinated and grilled for London broil, with one served for dinner and the other saved to top a Caesar salad later in the week. The remaining meat is cut up for beef stir-fry over brown rice. The fresh green beans on sale get used as a side dish for the first dinner, with some saved for the stir-fry later, too.

Substituting or skipping ingredients is another option. That flank steak in the grilled Caesar stands in for a rib eye. A fish dish with ginger, chiles, soy sauce, and sherry can call for red snapper all it wants, like some piscatorial Stanley Kowalski crying out for "Stella! Stella!," but I've made it with tilapia, it works great with catfish and, if you're in the right mood, the cheap, farm-raised salmon from Costco. The 99-cent package of manager's special hamburger buns can stand in for toast and sandwich bread this week. And the crème fraîche that's required for the lobster stew I mentioned earlier, at more than $5 for an 8-ounce container? That recipe is just fine without it (but don't rat me out to *The New York Times*, okay?).

Put it all together and, when it comes to grocery shopping, this is the low-hanging fruit (ha!) that can save you a lot of money without a lot of effort.

Making ends meet

You are going to have to make your peace with using coupons and realize you can do it without becoming the kind of crazy cat lady who spends whole days collecting them, then ties up the entire checkout line while she fishes out a fistful of newspaper clippings, half of them expired, and then spends a half hour arguing with the checkout clerk before trying to pay with a double-endorsed, third-party, out-of-state check.

You can spend no more than hour a week planning your shopping, breeze through the checkout, and save hundreds of dollars a month. If you need any more motivation, consider this: The Lexus ES 350, according to reviewers at Edmunds.com, is a car "for buyers who put the highest priority on comfort and luxury," with an overall level of opulence that offers "the utmost in refinement and relaxation."

Why do I mention this vehicle? Because of my friend, Doreen Christensen, the consumer reporter at the south Florida *Sun-Sentinel* and a woman who treats paying full price for anything the way Superman approaches Kryptonite. Doreen has a new Lexus ES 350, and she's paying for it with grocery coupons.

Doreen aims to cover her car payment each month with the money she saves by using coupons. In one impressive shopping excursion, she saved $450 on a cart stuffed with food and staples by combining coupons, store specials, and a little planning. As of March, she'd already saved enough to make the payments on her Lexus through September.

"People assume this is hard to do," Doreen says. "Just try it, and when you see how much you save, you'll be hooked. I'm not advocating stocking up a hundred bottles of syrup in your bedroom, but not using a dollar-off coupon would be like taking $1 and throwing it into the street."

To claim big savings, Doreen says you just need to take five steps.

First, sign up for loyalty or preferred customer discounts at your favorite grocery store and get on the mailing list for the weekly store flyers or other specials. If there's a rewards program that gives back money or discounts on gas, sign up for that, too. After all, gas and groceries are something most of us buy every week. For additional savings, look to see if your regular grocery store offers gas discounts with its loyalty card program, and look for online coupon offers that automatically work if you link them to your loyalty card.

If your store offers an e-coupon program that will send you coupons via e-mail or directly to your smartphone, sign up for that, too. I've added the Key Ring app to my smartphone, which stores my loyalty cards so that I can scan my phone screen at the checkout instead of cluttering up my key ring with a dozen of those annoying little pieces of plastic. The Key Ring app also automatically downloads special offers and exclusive coupons and links to weekly store flyers. CardStar is a similar app, and there's also an iPhone-only app called Passbook.

The next item in the coupon toolbox, Doreen says, is to get *two* copies of the Sunday newspaper (remember: gum disease!). You're only saving coupons for things you use, items that are free, and items that are buy one, get one free. The reason you want two of the newspaper coupons is because, hey, more coupons, and so you can combine them when you find a buy one, get one free (BOGO) sale at the store. Doreen explains, "If there are buy one, get one free sales you can use two manufacturer or store coupons, because you're buying two items. That's a very simple way to really double up your savings." And if you have a BOGO coupon from the manufacturer and find a BOGO sale at the store, use the coupon and get both items for free, plus tax. (Coupon policies vary from store to store, but most allow this tactic.)

Third, gather additional coupons from a few select sources. That includes online coupon sites, such as Coupons.com and Smart Source.com. If your grocery store honors competitors' coupons, either save inserts and flyers from other stores, or visit their Web sites, such as Target.com, for printable coupons. For more savings, search the Web for coupon match-up sites that pair your store's weekly specials with current coupons. It takes a little research and you have to figure out the difference between a "catalina" (coupons printed at the checkout register) and a "blinkie" (a small electronic device in store aisles with blinking lights that prints coupons for a nearby item), but, again, you are looking only for items you use or huge sales on something you'd substitute for a preferred brand. The Grocery Game also offers coupon matching.

Fourth, go to the manufacturer's Web site for brands you frequently buy, such as Kellogg's or Procter & Gamble. Besides finding printable coupons at those sites, you also can register for coupons or sign up for samples of products or brands you frequently use, and get coupons or even free samples of new products, which also usually come with additional coupons.

Lastly, don't forget social media. Going on Facebook to "like" your favorite brand or manufacturer also brings you additional coupons and samples. Sign up for freebies and special offers.

What you're looking to do is find a couple of coupon sources that will consistently work for you without a lot of time and hassle, so don't feel that you have to do this all at once. You can sample one or two match-up sites a week before you do your shopping instead of plowing through two dozen different sites on some kind of day-long extreme couponing bender. If you don't weigh every possible purchase but just look for things you already use, it will help cut down on your coupon-hunting time.

Come grocery-shopping time, you're looking to combine coupons with BOGOs or store specials. Or, if they're offered in your area, shop on double-coupon days, when stores will give you twice the face value of a coupon, making an offer of 50 cents off worth $1. You're also looking to combine or "stack" coupons, including competitor, store, and manufacturer coupons. Here's an example from Doreen: Atkins frozen entrées are normally $3.99. She combined a manufacturer's $1-off coupon with the store's buy one, get one free sale, meaning her twelve entrées cost $12 instead of $48. That's lunch for two weeks at $1 a day plus $36 toward her car payment.

Doreen estimates she spends about twenty minutes getting her list together and checking store flyers and coupons before shopping.

At the store, I sometimes have to search to find a sale item, which is often in a separate display, or to see whether the generic is still cheaper than a name brand with a 50-cents-off coupon. But it pays off.

"I got to the grocery store at 2:30 and I got home at 4 and I won't have to go back next week," Doreen said of a recent trip. "I spent $99 and saved $127. That's going to cover me for two weeks. Everything I bought was something I am going to use. By clipping coupons, I saved myself $127. I don't want to hand over that money to the grocery store."

Pinching pennies so hard that Lincoln gets a headache

The first step is to do the most with what you have. The Natural Resources Defense Council cites studies showing that American households waste $40 billion in food every year.[1] About 20 percent of that comes from vegetables and 15 percent from fruit, and I'm not surprised. At our house, the vegetable bin in the refrigerator always seems to contain some withered scallions, mushrooms turning to just mush, or an apple that's gone so bad it's about to start dating Charlie Sheen.

One solution is to shop more frequently for things that will spoil, since I always seem to overestimate how many vegetables I will eat, or end up with a whole head of lettuce but then only use a few leaves for a sandwich. Instead of shopping for vegetables all at once with a big coupon-laden money-saving trip, trim the veggie list and then hit the store midweek to refresh the dairy and vegetables as needed.

This means you need to keep just a short list, hit the perimeter of the store, where the veggies and milk are, and avoid the center aisles full of expensive snacks, treats, and soda. This can be hard if you have one or more children in tow, as when you hit the grocery store after picking up the kids from school. Suddenly, you find the cart filled with Oreos, Goldfish crackers, juice boxes, and other must-haves for the kids, or you end up arguing with and dragging a bunch of sullen, grumbling children through the store. With Li'l Money, I take one of two tactics: He can choose one thing and one thing only (subject to my approval), and that's it. Or I use this trick from my former editor, Mark "The Closer" Truby. If the grocery store is close to a dollar store, I tell the boy that if he helps me with the shopping and doesn't whine, beg, plead, scream, or otherwise complain, he can buy *anything* in the dollar store. For a mere $1.06 (with sales tax), I get a quick, peaceful shopping trip and he gets to make the dollar store his oyster.

Another option is to build meals around not only what's in your pantry but what's getting ready to turn in the fridge. That soon-to-wilt leftover lettuce dictates that tonight's dinner is a salad Niçoise, made with bargain tuna fish. Those fading zucchinis suggest a stir-fry, vegetable stock, or maybe some tasty but cheap zucchini latkes (the zucchini replaces the potatoes *and* it's healthier. Add applesauce and some turkey sausages and you are living, pal.).

Of course, vegetables aren't the only leftovers. My mom, raised during the Depression, would occasionally declare, "It's must go-down night." That meant that a backlog of small portions of leftovers, dated produce, or meat was piling up in the fridge and was going to be disposed of through us, her loving family, not the In-SinkErator. We'd pick from the smorgasbord of leftovers, with maybe a vegetable or side of mashed potatoes thrown in, and the world didn't come to an end just because we weren't all eating exactly the same thing.

Naturally, anything you can grow in your garden is nearly free, and things such as carrots, tomatoes, zucchini, beans of any type, and squash are pretty easy to cultivate. We grew three kinds of lettuce as well as some herbs in the Funny Money kitchen garden last year, and we had better salads than we could've bought for next to nothing all summer. My paternal grandfather, Frank O'Connor Sr., who raised ten kids during the Depression, rotated green beans, pole beans, and wax beans through his garden for the whole summer. There was one late July week that my brother and I stayed with Frank and Grandma Clara at the lake and I thought we were going to turn into beans.

Farmers' markets and food co-ops are other options to stretch a food budget, but they also demand that you adapt your menus to use what's cheap and in season. The way to really enjoy seasonal ingredients is to check out the recipes in your newspaper, or go online and find stories from places with really good food sections. My coworker Kate Lawson, *The Detroit News* food editor, comes up with dandy stuff over at DetroitNews.com every Thursday, and the City Kitchen column on *The New York Times* Web site always has something in season and terrific. If, for example, you see a nice bag of littleneck clams on sale at Costco, as I did recently, the City Kitchen recipe for clams and pasta is more than just the thing.[2]

Also, don't overlook U-pick farms, especially if you're into canning. Whether it's apples or blueberries, these kinds of outings can provide an afternoon's worth of outdoor activity as well. When my parents visited us in Florida during strawberry season, my mother and I spent one of our most memorable afternoons picking fresh strawberries and winter tomatoes at a place out on State Road 7. We hit the deli on the way home, which had just marked down a fresh batch of buffalo mozzarella. That evening we had a memorable meal that started with insalata Caprese and ended with strawberries and whipped cream over fresh drop biscuits. It might have been cheap, but it tasted like a million bucks.

Another low-cost option is to stretch what you're cooking. I first learned this technique from my Sarah Lawrence College pal Laurie Lytel, who is now Nevada's finest family therapist. Laurie bought frozen orange juice and, instead of adding three cans of water, threw in four. Voilà—one more day of juice for free! Extend that technique by adding more rice, vegetables, or noodles to turn a recipe that serves six into one that serves eight. I routinely double up the amount of tomatoes and onions in my chili and any ground beef casserole, and the extra vitamin C and fiber goes does us all good. And for real bargain recipes (plus many more tips, coupon links, and more) I like to scan 5dollardinners.com, which even offers a weekly meal planner. Make a double batch and freeze the leftovers.

Of course, if you are in a dire situation you should absolutely take advantage of any food assistance programs you can find. Right now, we have more people on food stamps in this country than on unemployment, so don't hesitate to see if you qualify, even if you've got a job. Also look for food pantries in your area by checking with United Way and local social service agencies and churches.

If you want to go really hard-core to save on food, you can raise rabbits or chickens, but consider the hassle, neighbors, zoning laws, and your own squeamishness. Dolly Freed's very interesting book *Possum Living* details her experience living on next to no income, in part by relying on a steady supply of home-raised rabbit meat.[3] In her informative and entertaining *Make the Bread, Buy the Butter*, Jennifer Reese gives details and recipes based on her own experience after losing a job and deciding to find out just when homemade beats store-bought, and vice versa.[4] Once you've made your own guacamole you'll never go back—and you'll save money. Just make sure you don't spend it all on beer when you invite your friends over to sample your killer guac.

The Bottom Line

Goal: $1,000

Week 1—Transportation . . . $41.61
Week 2—Miscellaneous . . . $132.89
Week 3—Utilities . . . $139.39
Week 4—Kid Costs . . . $114.50
Week 5—Work Expenses . . . $90
Week 6—Personal Spending . . . $104
Week 7—Entertainment . . . $108
Week 8—Life Insurance . . . $64.40
Week 9—Groceries . . . $37.23
Total monthly savings . . . $832.02

Left to cut . . . $167.98

According to my budget, living expenses ate up to 10 percent of our family income, and two-thirds of that was groceries. But trying to shrink the grocery bill showed that saving on food was going to come in nibbles, not big bites, leaving me far short of the week's $100 goal.

I found the Grocery Game easy to use. It took about a half hour of planning, as well as some tromping around the store to find the sale items. But our savings after four weeks weren't very dramatic—$37.23 for the month, though we added a lot of items to the freezer and pantry. As Gault noted, savings at the start are low until Grocery Game users go through a full cycle of savings.

We'd already been cutting back on food and other supermarket sundries, buying paper goods in bulk at a warehouse club, splurging on premium steaks only when they were on a big sale, and switching mostly to store brands and generics for everything else.

"It doesn't surprise me that you're not saving a lot yet, because you were already a good saver," Gault said. "What you're doing is amassing things you'll use beyond the next twelve weeks. After that, your needs are basically just your produce and milk and replenishing your investments."

That's encouraging, and I had talked to one Metro Detroiter who did, indeed, slash her supermarket spending by 50 percent with the Grocery Game. But at the moment my attempt at cutting the food budget left a bitter taste in my mouth. It also left $167.98 in savings I had to find in my last category: housing.

Forget raccoon. It looked like I was going to end up eating crow.

$ 11

Housing

You Can't Drive Your House, but You Can
Live in Your Car, and at Least Then You Won't
Have to Deal with a Property Appraisal

The final week of The $1,000 Challenge came the week of Christmas, thus introducing a new, short-lived holiday tradition. Besides the decking of the halls and the caroling of the choirs, I had the hassling of the mortgage. If that's not part of your holiday observance, count yourself lucky. If it is, then you added the rare Christmas Eve tradition of listening not for the prancing and pawing of reindeer on the roof but for the call of the real estate appraiser.

That decidedly nonjoyous strain echoed as though on high because the last column in my cost-cutting series covered trying to refinance my mortgage. To make the project's $1,000 goal, I was looking to slice nearly $170 out of the house payment, including insurance, taxes, and maintenance. Refinancing the mortgage seemed the best bet to save the kind of dough I needed to find. After all, housing costs are the top budget category for most families, soaking up more than a quarter of all gross income. If there was anywhere to save, I thought it ought to be here.

Maybe it was, but there was no way I was going to find out anytime soon.

Thanks to the mortgage mania that put us in the recession, all kinds of rules have been added to a simple home refinancing, especially the appraisal. My first step was to gather recommendations for local mortgage brokers. I found one that didn't charge an application fee until an appraisal had been conducted, so that I wouldn't waste $400 or $500 in nonrefundable application fees on top of a $300 appraisal bill if my home's value didn't qualify for a new loan.

I calculated that refinancing my 5.5 percent mortgage to 4.875 percent, and rolling the balance of a small variable rate home equity line, would have cut $113 from my monthly housing cost.

I badly need to score the savings, which would put me within 60 bucks of my $1,000 goal. So I got the mortgage broker to tell her manager to tell the independent third-party appraisal management firm to tell the independent real estate appraiser that I needed the appraisal before Christmas. They all put a big "rush" on the job—which was then scheduled to be delivered on January 4, weeks after my final column. That meant I needed to look elsewhere for the week's savings.

My other housing costs didn't offer much hope either. My insurance and taxes were already low, but I did cut the maid service to once a month, which saved $60. If I trained the dust bunnies to march in formation, I thought, maybe Mrs. Funny Money and I could charge admission, or even take the show on the road. That still left me with more than $100 to cut from my budget. I was going to have to keep looking—but where?

Freeing up cash

Since my budget-cutting experiment, interest rates have only gone down, thanks to our sucktastic economy and the weak "recovery" that continues to be hobbled, in large part, by the ongoing crisis of foreclosures and drastically lowered home values, which even in early 2013 remain off their peak by more than 30 percent in much of the country. That means anyone who bought a house after fall of 2003 probably owes more on their mortgage than their home is worth. (As of March, anyone in Metro Detroit who bought after the summer of 1996 has likely lost money.)

If you can swing a refinancing and rates haven't risen too high, it can be worth it. With mortgage rates hovering around 3.60 percent during the first quarter of 2013, that left homeowners paying just slightly above the average annual 3 percent rate of inflation to borrow money for three decades. In other words, even at low inflation rates, in just a few years you'll be paying back the loan with money that's cheaper than it is today. The savings on a $100,000, 5.5 percent loan refinanced to 3.6 percent is more than $110 off your monthly payment, or more than $40,000 in saved interest during the life of the loan. Another reason to refinance is if you have an adjustable-rate loan. The rate may be less than the going rates on fixed-term loans now, but you'd be wise to refi and lock in a permanently low rate before your loan adjusts above the current low rates. Some adjustable loans will let you lock in a fixed rate at some point during your loan, so check that option first, since you'll avoid the costs of refinancing. It'll probably be quicker, too.

Before you refinance, you have to deal with two questions: Can you afford it? And, if so, can you qualify for a new loan?

Whether you can afford a refinance comes down to how much you'll save and how long it will take for the savings to cover your new loan costs. The rules to keep in mind for a modern-day refinancing are simple: it should not lengthen the term of the loan; it should pay for itself in twenty-four months or less; and, other than loan fees, it should not raise your loan balance. Personally, I try to pay cash for the cost of refinancing rather than roll the costs into the new loan because I don't want to add more debt and end up paying interest—no matter how low—on the refinancing charges for the next ten or twenty years.

So, get out your calculator and a scratch pad and . . .

Do the math: First, figure out how much you'll be able to save, maybe using the mortgage and refi calculators at Bank-rate.com.[1] If you're five years into a $150,000 thirty-year loan, the monthly savings on switching from a rate of 5.5 percent to 4 percent for the remaining twenty-five years comes to $93 a month.

Do some more math: Total up the fees and other refinancing costs and figure out your break-even point. If, using the example above, it costs $1,800 to refinance, you'd make your money back in less than twenty months. If it will take too long to recoup your outlay, look for a loan with no points and no costs. Your lowest-cost bet will often be to refinance with your current lender, especially if you haven't had the loan for a long time. If the property surveys and other paperwork aren't too old, some lenders won't require new documents, which makes the refinancing process faster and cheaper.

Fix your rate: For most people, there's no reason to monkey around with adjustable-rate or interest-only loans. Lower fixed rates virtually erase the "savings" from those kinds of gimmicky loans. The savings on a fixed-rate loan at 3.6 percent versus an adjustable mortgage at 2.68 percent where the rate is fixed for five years and then adjusts annually (a 5/1 adjustable-rate mortgage, or ARM) comes out to $72 a month. If that's the sole difference in being able to afford a refi, then you might want to skip it. Even if you do recoup the costs in the first few years, you'll certainly be paying higher rates when the loan starts adjusting after the initial fixed period. If, however, the increase is capped and you won't stay in the house all that long (most of us move about every ten years, on average), then an ARM can work for you. Just be sure that you understand exactly how high your loan can adjust in any one year and during the life of the loan, and make sure it will be affordable at those levels.

Think long-term: Shop for a mortgage banker or broker the same way you shop for a mechanic: you need someone you trust who's been in business for many years and will be there for more years to come. As I suggested earlier, try to find someone who will arrange to have your home appraised before charging a loan application fee. That way if the home's value doesn't qualify, you won't lose the application fee.

An important step in refinancing is to avoid lengthening the term of your loan. If you're already several years into a thirty-year mortgage, going back to start over with another thirty-year loan will add all those years of interest back onto your new mortgage. Even if your monthly payment is lower, your total cost is going to be higher. And because mortgages are front-loaded to pay mostly interest at the beginning of the loan, you'll owe more on the balance of your refinanced loan after five years than you did on the original, higher-rate mortgage.

Assuming a refinance makes sense, the next step is to find out if you'll qualify for a new loan. Lenders have drastically tightened up their underwriting standards since the bursting of the mortgage bubble, even insisting on radical notions like finding out how much money you make and whether you'll actually be able to repay the loan.

The first step is your credit score. Anything around 720 (out of 850 points) or higher will get you the best rates, while anything below 620 means you're unlikely to obtain a new mortgage at even the worst rates. You aren't entitled to a free copy of your credit score, but you can get a free estimate on the Web. Bankrate.com has a good estimator,[2] or buy your score from Fair Isaac Corporation, the folks who invented the credit score.[3] Don't go anywhere else, and don't sign up for "free" credit monitoring or other services because there is no such thing, no matter what the singing pirates told you in that TV ad.

Your mortgage broker will, in all likelihood, run a credit score on you, too, and you should be wary of anyone who quotes you a set rate before at least asking about your credit history. If your score is marginal there are steps you can take to boost your score in just a few months. The biggest one is to make every single credit payment on time, since that counts for the biggest single portion of your credit score. You also can move around your credit card balances, raise your credit limits, and take other steps that will help improve this mystical, magical credit talisman. For more information, head back to the discussion of credit scores under "Insurance" in chapter 2 or get a copy of *Your Credit Score, Your Money & What's at Stake*, by Liz Weston.[4]

The next step is determining whether you owe more on your home than its current appraised value. If the ratio of the loan amount to the value of the home is 80 percent or less, you're a good candidate for a refi with lots of lenders, so go shop around. (Here's the math: LOAN AMOUNT divided by HOME VALUE = your loan-to-value ratio.) If the loan-to-value ratio (or LTV, in mortgage-speak) is 97 percent or less, you may find refinancing available, but you'll likely have to pay for additional private mortgage insurance. If you're north of 100 percent and are current on your payments, your options are to see if your lender will refinance the home, or look to refinance under the Home Affordable Refinance Program (HARP). HARP, which started in 2009, got off to a shaky start, but it has been reworked to become HARP 2.0, which eliminated any limit on the loan-to-value amount. New legislation means more adjustments came to HARP in 2013.

The big drawback to HARP is that it covers only loans owned by the government-backed mortgage insurers Fannie Mae and Freddie Mac before June 1, 2009. (You can check your loan online at fanniemae.com[5] or by calling 800-732-6643, or at freddiemac.com[6] or by calling 800-373-3343.) A separate refinance program, called the FHA Streamline, is available for homeowners with FHA loans. If you don't have a loan through Fannie Mae, Freddie Mac, or the FHA, still try local mortgage brokers and your own lender and servicer, since the policies and guidelines seem to shift every few months. You also should check with a HUD-certified housing counselor. You can find the list at HUD.gov[7] or by calling 888-995-4673.

If you have a second mortgage, home equity line of credit, or home equity loan, that can complicate a refinance, since that lender will also have to sign off on the new mortgage. This is less of a problem if you have the equity loan with the same lender as the mortgage or if you have enough equity to refinance both loans under the new mortgage. Another option is to see if you can do the refi through the lender who owns the equity loan or second mortgage.

A final option for some homeowners who owe more than their property is worth is what's called a "cash-in" refi. Instead of taking cash out of the home, you bring cash to the closing to pay the mortgage balance down to an acceptable loan-to-value ratio. This isn't going to be the right approach unless you've got your finances in good shape, with no other major debt and a solid emergency fund. It can make sense if you're on the bubble and just shy of getting down to a qualifying loan-to-value rate or if you've got a lot of cash sitting around that you're sick of seeing earn practically nothing in a bank account. Cashing in is also an option to wipe out a home equity loan so that you can refinance the first mortgage.

Two final caveats: So-called no-cost refis aren't free; they just charge a slightly higher rate to cover the closing costs. Also, a refinance that lowers your interest will also lower the amount of interest you'll be able to deduct on your taxes next year. Don't assume your deductions will be the same; check the interest using any online loan amortization calculator and see how that might change your tax withholding using the very nifty withholding calculator at IRS.gov.[8]

Making ends meet

First, look over all the elements of your house payment and see if you can lower or eliminate any of them. Typically, house payments include principal and interest on the loan, but also taxes and insurance, which you pay into an escrow fund. Even if you pay them yourself, insurance and taxes are still part of your overall housing cost. Start with your homeowners insurance. You can lower the deductible, eliminate some optional riders, and shop the policy around to see if you can save on the premium. Check to see if you got something like mortgage life insurance, which pays off the mortgage if you die. This is usually more limited and more expensive than buying good basic term insurance, as discussed in chapter 9.

The next step is looking at your tax bill. In the very likely event that the value of your house has dropped in the past several years, your municipality's assessment of the value of your property should have been lowered, too, resulting in a smaller tax bill for you. But especially in hard times, local assessors may take a conservative view toward lowering assessments in order to keep tax revenue coming in. Procedures to challenge your assessment vary by state.

In Michigan, I go to a board in my town, and if I want to appeal their decision, I have a limited window to take it to a state panel. Some local tax specialists have made a practice out of handling these appeals, and I could hire one starting at $100. You'll have to check with your local assessor and perhaps the state treasurer's office to see how things work where you live. For the most part, it's an investment of time, researching recent comparable sales in your area, and doing a little homework to submit an appeal based on what your property is really worth. Your final tax bill is based on a certain charge per each $1,000 of taxable value on your house, so you can calculate any potential savings with some simple multiplication. If you shave $20,000 off your taxable value and your tax rate ("mileage") is $5 per $1,000, you'll trim your tax bill by $100 a year (20,000 divided by 1,000, times $5).

Another mortgage option you can afford to dump, if you use it, is a biweekly mortgage program. These are programs that, for a fee, take half your mortgage payment every two weeks so that, by the end of the year, you've made twenty-six half-payments, resulting in an extra thirteenth full payment on your mortgage each year. This prepaying can knock several years off a thirty-year mortgage. But you can do it yourself for free, and you don't need to tie up a big wad of your money every two weeks. Instead, put one-twelfth of your monthly payment aside in a savings account each month, and then send in the extra payment yourself when you've got a thirteenth payment built up. That way, you have the money available if you need it. Which, at this point, you do. If you were saving separately this way you could easily take the money out and stop paying into it each month. If you're in a biweekly payment program and you cancel it, you'll get more control over your monthly cash flow as well as cut out any fees you pay for the privilege of prepaying your own home loan.

In fact, you shouldn't be prepaying your mortgage at all if you are barely getting by, have debt, have no emergency savings, or aren't saving adequately for retirement. Prepaying your tax-deductible, usually low-rate mortgage is pretty much the last thing you should do if you have any other financial concerns. Partly this is because you lose the opportunity to compound investments for retirement. If you're sending extra money to your mortgage that could go into your workplace 401(k) or similar plan and be matched by your employer, you could be losing out on free money from your employer match that will also compound over time. (Even if you don't receive a match, you're still missing the gains from compounding over time.) Worst of all, whatever money you prepay on your mortgage is tied up in your house, making it very hard to get at it if you run into financial problems, or impossible if you don't have any equity.

You may be offered or decide to pursue a mortgage modification, which is where your mortgage servicer reduces your interest rate or, in rare cases, even the amount of the principal. While some servicers have their own programs, the big one is the U.S. Treasury backed Home Affordable Modification Program (HAMP). However, if you apply, you need to be very, very careful. In my reporting, I've found many homeowners who ended up worse off because of HAMP, and many were pushed into foreclosure and ruined because of servicer greed and incompetence and pathetically poor government oversight. HAMP has recently been subjected to more rules, and the new Consumer Finance Protection Bureau has jumped in to rein in the worst mortgage-servicing abuses, but you should still proceed with great caution in pursuing a modification.

You can wind up with two problems, which occur during the "trial" phase of a modification, where your monthly payments are temporarily lowered. If you make them successfully, you are supposed to get your modification made permanent, but many homeowners get turned down, often because the servicer will make more money on a bad trial modification and a foreclosure. According to the Obama administration's own statistics, more homeowners have been kicked out of "trial" modifications than have received permanent ones. (Housing experts estimate another 800,000 homeowners were improperly turned down completely, a lucky break for many of them who avoided the horrors of a busted "trial" modification.)

The problem is that during your "trial" payment period, your servicer is likely to report your payments as late to the credit bureaus, which is going to ruin your credit, especially when a "trial" stretches beyond three months to six months or even a year or more. The other thing is that when the modification is denied, the servicer can demand the balance of all your temporarily lowered payments, along with added fees and late charges. If you don't cough up all that cash right away, the servicer can (and often will) initiate foreclosure proceedings. In some cases, the additional balance gets added onto the end of the existing loan term, still leaving you worse off than when you started.

The added insult is that applying for a HAMP modification isn't easy. Servicers frequently lose paperwork, misdirect phone calls, fail to respond, give out incorrect information, and require multiple submissions of pay stubs, tax returns, and other documents. Much of it is handled by fax, phone, and express mail, since e-mail is unheard-of during the process. In some cases servicers "dual track" a loan in modification, meaning that they are seeking to foreclose or may have already started foreclosure even while "trial" modification payments are being made.

Some people, though, have gotten significant modifications, especially if they had high-rate mortgages to begin with. If you have the wherewithal to churn through the paperwork and red tape required for a modification, keep good written records and write down the full name of anyone you deal with and the date on which you talked. Send any documents by certified mail, and whenever you're given new information or told to make a change, send a letter spelling out your understanding of what's happening and what is being told to you by whom. Keep copies. As the process drags on, expect to send in new documents such as pay stubs and tax statements. If the ones previously submitted become outdated (usually more than ninety days old), the servicer may use that as an excuse to deny your modification, often without requesting newer ones.

If you get a "trial" modification, bank the difference in a separate account so that you have the money on hand if your "trial" mod is denied. Also, before accepting a modification, find out exactly how the lowered payments will be reported to credit bureaus and weigh the risk to your credit. Try to work with a HUD-certified housing counselor, and don't listen to anyone who says that you must be delinquent on your loan to qualify, which isn't true for owner-occupied homes. Starting out sixty days late when you request the modification is very likely to trigger the foreclosure process.

Pinching pennies so hard that Lincoln gets a headache

As discussed earlier, refinancing into a new thirty-year mortgage, even if you are already several years into your current loan, costs more in the long run and sets you back in building equity in your home. But, if you're really pressed and a refi will significantly lower your monthly payment, it's worth considering to get the short-term relief now. Later, when your financial situation improves, you can consider prepaying your mortgage principal to lower your overall interest cost and catch up on equity, if that's appropriate. But first consider other options, even if it means leaving the home. If staying and refinancing does make sense, you'll likely want to roll as much of the refi cost into the new loan as possible, but you'll also need to come up with a certain amount of cash. Make sure you've got enough cash available before you start laying out money for application fees and other refi expenses.

Less expensive options for lowering your cost of housing include renting out a room, ideally to someone you know, such as a friend or the child of a relative attending school nearby or a summer intern from work. Just how and with whom you want to share your home is a very personal choice, but make sure you arrange this as a business deal first and foremost. Spell out all the terms beforehand and in writing and use a state-approved lease. Also try a short-term rental at first to see whether this kind of thing is going to be comfortable for you. You may also want to run a background and credit check on your potential tenants.

If you want to be strictly legal about things, income you get from renting your home is taxable, but you can also deduct a share of your mortgage, interest, and other housing expenses to offset the tax. You also need to check your local laws on renting, or at least gauge whether your neighbors will complain when you suddenly take a family of four into your spare bedroom. You should check with your insurance agent to make sure you're covered and, if possible, have any long-term renters take out their own rental insurance to cover their own personal property and liability.

A more drastic option is to rent out your entire house while you move somewhere less expensive, such as in with a relative. This is going to be more complicated, and you may want to consult with a property manager who can handle the details, unless you really want to be a landlord, which you probably don't. Depending on the circumstances, there can be significant risks and hassles involved in renting your home, not the least of which is that the rent you charge might not cover your entire monthly payment for mortgage, insurance, and taxes. But it is one way to hang on to a home that you can't refinance until your financial situation improves or until the market value increases and you can sell or refinance the home.

Selling the home and moving to something cheaper is another possibility, but it also comes with its own set of costs and hassles, including cleaning up your home to make it marketable, finding a listing agent, and bearing the cost of finding and moving to a new place. You can try a short sale if you just want to get out from under a home you can no longer afford, which is where your lender agrees to let you sell the home for less than what you owe. This involves all the cost and hassle of a regular sale, plus more, which I'm sure is just what's missing from your life.

It can take up to six months or longer to get your lender's approval for a short sale when you finally get an offer. Also be aware that a short sale will significantly lower your credit score, so line up any new loans and living arrangements beforehand, since landlords will check your score before renting. A short sale is also likely to make it difficult to qualify for a new mortgage for the next several years, with a three-year wait after a short sale required to qualify for an FHA loan. Finally, a short sale doesn't necessarily mean you don't still owe the full amount to your lender. Unless you get a specific release for the deficiency between what was owed and the price for which the property sold, your lender may be able to pursue you for the balance for years to come, with interest added. In some cases, lenders have required sellers to take out a personal loan for the unpaid balance. Banks have become much more willing to consider short sales in the last few years, however, because it is better for them than having you default and let the house go into foreclosure. Before starting the process consult a real estate agent with considerable short-sale experience, as well as a real estate attorney experienced with short sales, to protect yourself against a really big claim later.

Whatever you do, don't fall for one of the many schemes and scams that prey on desperate homeowners, where middlemen promise they can help you "save" your house. The legitimate ones are of dubious value at best, and many are outright scams. You should be especially wary of anyone who wants to take your payment instead of having you send it to the lender, as well as anyone who wants to be paid up front. Various schemes that promise to "wipe out" your debts are a fraud, and offers to buy your house and lease it back to you are very risky at best, and most are cons designed to take both your house and your money. Do not, under any conditions, sign over your deed or a quitclaim deed without talking to your own attorney first. For a list of home-saving scams, check out the warnings from the Office of the Comptroller of the Currency at OCC.gov.[9]

If your finances are really in turmoil, none of this may help, and you need to consider, rationally and dispassionately, whether you can realistically afford your house. If your income has taken a huge hit, you have no significant assets other than retirement accounts, and you've been unemployed for a long time, the prospects of being able to keep making your house payment are dim. If you are already behind on your payments, they're even worse. But as bad as things are, you can get yourself into even more trouble by trying to keep your home.

Many homeowners, hoping that a miracle—or at least a job—will come through, drain their family resources to try and keep a home or struggle through a trial modification. That includes taking money out of retirement accounts or borrowing from relatives, often using up assets that can be protected in bankruptcy. The upshot is that struggling homeowners deplete all their resources and still lose their homes, leaving them with no money to find a new place to live and putting their retirement and future finances at risk.

If you cannot make your home payment, start with a certified debt counselor and/or HUD-approved housing counselor from the list at HUD.gov.[10] Also contact an experienced consumer bankruptcy attorney, preferably one with foreclosure experience. You want someone who has been handling bankruptcies for years, not just a lawyer who switched over to bankruptcies when the economy turned sour. I've seen some terrible advice handed out by otherwise good attorneys who were inexperienced with personal bankruptcy and foreclosure. If your attorney thinks it's okay, contact the mortgage lender or servicer, who may offer you "cash for keys," paying you a few thousand to move out quickly and leave the home in good condition.

As difficult a step as this is to consider, make sure you weigh all your options before spending every last dime trying to hang on to what is, despite your understandable attachment to it, just a piece of property. Your long-term responsibility is to provide for yourself and your family. In Michigan, for example, foreclosed homeowners have a six-month redemption period after the sheriff's sale of the property during which they can redeem the property if they raise the money. It's also six months to stay in the home, save up as much cash as possible, sell off your appliances, and find another place to live. During this time, keep paying the insurance (to protect yourself) and the minimum to keep the lights, water, and heat on, save your money, and make your plans to move forward in life. It will be unpleasant, to say the least, but take comfort in doing the right thing for you and your family and that you certainly aren't alone.

Boat and miscellaneous

The shortfall from my delayed refinancing meant I had to expand into some more budget categories. I scanned down to the eleventh-largest category of our family spending, which was the Funny Money family fleet. This amateur armada consisted of a thirty-year-old deck boat that was paid for but needed repairs all the time, often sinking the monthly budget. We had also been hanging onto its slightly older twin, which had died a year before but which, on the advice of our mechanic, Big Tom, we kept for parts.

You may not have a boat, in which case, good for you, because you don't have to spend the last weekend in October sloshing around in borrowed chest waders pulling your dock out of forty-degree water because you're too cheap to pay for a dock service and your wife insists on getting every last Indian summer weekend of use out of your vessel.

But certainly you will have expenses beyond your ten largest spending categories, so if you can't hit your savings goal by cutting the biggest things, start looking through the less-big things in your budget. Maybe it's a snowmobile, a recreational vehicle, or an expensive hobby (such as competing in extreme dog grooming) that involves equipment that regularly breaks down, blows up, or otherwise creates unexpected maintenance issues. Whatever it is, cutting out unnecessary expenditures and setting up a budgeted monthly amount for maintenance, improvements, and supplies can smooth out the unexpected expenses that will show up to sink your budget without warning

The first boating expense I could cut was paying to store the old boat, which had to go. The storage bill was paid until spring, and after that Big Tom and I would pull off the parts we wanted, scrap the rest, and sell the trailer.

I also need to budget more consistently for repairs. In the previous year, my boat-related expenditures averaged a surprising $244.38 a month, a number that included the dock fee and several trips to the mechanic that left me digging deep into my next paycheck. Instead of coming up with money each time the boat breaks down, it would work better to budget for repairs and annual fees, then set that money aside each month in a separate savings account. With a boat built in 1979, unused repair money won't go unused for long. Any excess cash can build up from year to year to provide a cushion for occasions like last summer, when several fixes were needed. That way we can keep the aging SS *Money Pit* on the water without floating a credit card balance or sinking the family budget.

Making ongoing payments to a reserve fund for any kind of big annual expense, or to cover maintenance or repairs, is really a form of self-insuring for when the bilge pump breaks or when the boat prop and I manage to find that low spot in the channel with all the rocks (again). I averaged out the last three years of boat repairs, plus annual fees for docking and registration, and found that I could keep an adequate boat reserve fund going for $145 a month. (I guess I could call it a sinking fund, but that would just be tempting fate.) This produced savings of $99.38 and got me tantalizingly close to my final $1,000 savings goal—less than $9 short. So where else could I save?

Home maintenance

Back to the home front, it turned out that our monthly home maintenance and repair budget had also become inflated because, like the boat, there were a few big one-time expenses the previous year. Instead of the $100 per month we average in most years, the previous year worked out to more than $250 a month, boosting the repair and maintenance average over the past few years to $135 a month. Trimming that to $125 and accruing the difference in the annual expense/repairs account meant I could cut another $10 a month and still build an adequate reserve fund to cover big things.

The Bottom Line

Goal: $1,000

Week 1—Transportation . . . $41.61
Week 2—Miscellaneous . . . $132.89
Week 3—Utilities . . . $139.39
Week 4—Kid Costs . . . $114.50
Week 5—Work Expenses . . . $90
Week 6—Personal Spending . . . $104
Week 7—Entertainment . . . $108
Week 8—Life Insurance . . . $64.40
Week 9—Groceries . . . $37.23
Week 10—Housing . . . $169.38
Total monthly savings . . . $1,001.40

Wait—was I done? I'd made it—just barely—past the project's $1,000 goal, but only by cutting into an eleventh category, including $60 cut from maid service, $99.38 from boat maintenance, and $10 from home maintenance. It brought the final week's savings to

$169.38, just enough to put me an entire $1.40 over The $1,000 Challenge goal. And I may have saved even more. Mrs. Funny Money and I still were waiting to see bigger savings on life insurance premiums, the new grocery shopping plan, and, if the appraisal ever got done, the eventual home refinancing.

I waited for the heavens to open and a choir of angels to beam down in a shaft of sunlight above my paper-strewn desk, strumming the "Ode to Joy" on their golden harps. Nothing. Not even the Tooth Fairy playing "Pennies from Heaven" on a plastic kazoo. Nonetheless, I breathed a sigh of relief. My editors breathed a sigh of relief. And Mrs. Funny Money—who had been oh, so terribly thrilled to have the details of our family finances spread all over the hometown paper each week—breathed a very big sigh of relief.

In a few months, all that extra breathing room in the Funny Money family budget was a lifesaver—and not just for me. The credit card balances shrank, the speech specialists got paid, and a weekend anniversary trip wasn't out of the question. When a woodchuck burrowed under the foundation of the house, we could even afford to hire a "wildlife relocation specialist." He set his trap, then returned the next day to find it occupied—by a raccoon.

"What do you want me to do with him?" the trapper asked.

I looked over the raccoon's fat, furry haunches and tried to channel the spirit of Glemie Dean Beasley, Motown's favorite raccoon roaster.

I called back to the kitchen, "Honey, what's for dinner?"

"I'm getting a roast out of the freezer," Mrs. Funny Money answered.

So I let the furry little bandit loose. As I watched him scamper off toward the lake at least one of us, I knew, felt like the luckiest critter in Detroit.

$ Conclusion

So, what have learned in our journey through this useful and witty tome?

A. To save the most cash as quickly as possible, focus on your largest recurring expenses and examine every alternative, from the simplest to the most radically ruthless.
B. Don't spend money to save money.
C. Reading printed newspapers (*especially The Detroit News*) helps prevent gum disease. (For best results, wrap each day's front page around the handle of a Sonicare toothbrush used daily. Wait—didn't I mention that part before?)
D. Your results will—and should—vary.

It's been about four years since I concluded my ten-week series of cost-cutting columns, which means I've saved my family nearly $48,000 since then. Which is not say that I've got a huge stash of cash set aside, but we have had money to tackle everything from woodchuck eradication to colonoscopies. So, yeah, the good times are indeed rolling at the Funny Money house.

We've also had the wherewithal to handle those situations when a little-known automotive widget—the excess funds sensor—is triggered in one of our cars. If you've never heard of the excess funds sensor, or EFS for short, it is an extremely sensitive device that triggers a major malfunction of your vehicle any time the sensor discerns an unexpected positive balance in your bank account. For example, the receipt of a $900 tax refund is guaranteed to activate the EFS and result in a corresponding $1,100 transmission repair.

Which is all to say that anything in life is going to cost more and take longer than you expect, including just going about your daily life while trying to avoid debt, save for the future, and not be forced to drink the cheap Scotch. Money may not buy happiness, but it buys a heckuva lot more than being broke. Having a little extra money is the difference between walking home in the rain or being able to call AAA when your car breaks down. If nothing else, having some money means that when the tree branch crashes through your roof some windy night, even if you can't afford the repair, at least you can cover the hole with the really good blue tarp.

If I have learned anything from this experiment, it's that success in managing your household budget is defined by having more months than not when you hit a close approximation of your goal. Nonetheless, stick to it. The point isn't to reach penny-pinching perfection but to make sure that whatever you spend is money you really do need to spend, and that when you spend it, you're getting the best value available. If you end this month saving $1 more than last month, you're making progress, so don't take it as a personal failing that gas went up 30 cents a gallon this week. Monitor your results, change your tactics, and, when necessary, adjust your expectations. To say that budgeting isn't a science but an art is a drastic understatement. The truth is that budgeting is a really inexact and sloppy art, like trying to re-create *The Last Supper* out of chili cheese fries.

Nonetheless, I can truthfully report that every penny of savings I've described in this book was genuine and that Mrs. Funny Money and I acted right away on at least 90 percent of all the cost-cutting opportunities we found. A few moves were delayed for a while, such as repricing our life insurance coverage until we settled some health issues, or waiting to empty the old junk out of the garage and basement before we could cancel the storage unit and refill the garage and basement with new old junk.

For the most part, we've been able to stick with the bulk of the budgeting moves we started nearly four years ago. The utility bills and miscellaneous expenses have stayed down, and we save even more on auto expenses since Mrs. Funny Money stopped working nights, which allows us to ride together on two of the three days she heads downtown. There's been some backsliding at times, admittedly, especially on grocery shopping, since planning and doing a big grocery run every week or two is almost as much fun for Florida-bred Mrs. Funny Money as an ice-fishing trip in January.

Still, in any relationship there is bound to be some friction—real or imagined—when it comes to putting your saving strategies into practice. A few months ago I found whole chickens on sale and stocked up with four, planning to roast one for my dinner while Mrs. Funny Money was out working for the evening. Then I realized that roasting one was as much work as roasting all of them and decided to do all four at once. We don't own four roasting pans, so I opted for beer-can roasting, which involves sitting on a beer can partly inserted into the cavity between the legs (of the chickens).

I arranged a chorus line of fowl in the oven and roasted away, with all the birds turning out beautifully. I packed up the extras, washed out the beer cans for recycling, and headed off to bed, impressed with my own culinary and budgeting prowess. So I was dismayed the next morning when I was greeted with a baleful eye and an icy, accusatory tone after Mrs. Funny Money poured her coffee and noticed the stack of cans on the counter.

"Looks like you had yourself quite the little party last night," she sneered.

I eventually persuaded Mrs. Funny Money that her husband had spent the evening filling the freezer instead of emptying most of a cheap six-pack. The only thing that really convinced her? The fact that I'd used an off-brand beer instead of an expensive German import clearly proved that the brew went into the birds, not me.

Which brings us, in a way, to the moral of this whole book: if you buy East Toledo Pigswill Lager Lite for your cheap chickens, you can afford the good stuff for yourself.

Acknowledgments

I want to thank my editor at Portfolio, Maria Gagliano, for giving me the one thing each and every newspaper writer truly needs: money. By that, I mean having enough faith in my ideas and ability to give me a big-time publishing contract so that I might see my work lining the shelves of America's remaining major bookstores (both of them). In addition, I can't thank Maria enough for her deft and sure editing of my manuscript. Also, for the money.

That same thanks goes to my agent, Sam Fleishman of Literary Artists Agency, who resurrected the idea for this book and, thanks to his own very great enthusiasm, talent, and book biz savvy, landed us a deal in just six weeks, even after this book proposal had languished for two years. Also, Sam handles the money.

Another agent, my friend Lori Perkins, provided invaluable insight into the world of publishing in person, via Twitter, and through her book *The Insider's Guide to Getting an Agent*. New School writing teacher, author, and consultant (and former fifth-grade girlfriend) Sue Shapiro also provided invaluable guidance and encouragement, as did her husband, the very gracious and witty Charlie Rubin.

I also have to mention the late *Wall Street Journal* columnist Jeff Zaslow, who first encouraged me to pursue the idea for this book. The inspiration to turn my original "Grand Experiment" columns into something more came from Terri Thompson, director of the prestigious Knight-Bagehot Fellowship in business at Columbia University's Graduate School of Journalism. I can still hear her shout, "This should be a book!" when she called to tell me that I'd won the Christopher J. Welles Memorial Prize for the "Grand Experiment" columns, and that sense of excitement kept me plugging away at this project, even when few others seemed to shared her enthusiasm.

At *The Detroit News*, I have to thank Mark Truby and Don Nauss for making me a columnist in the first place and who, with Sue Burzynski Bullard, championed a column that must have been something quite a bit different from what they expected. I want to thank publisher Jon Wolman for his strong support and for allowing me to reuse some material from my columns, and Michael Brown for arranging all the legal details. I also want to thank Sue Carney for backing the original "Grand Experiment" series, and Joanna Firestone for continuing to support the column. Mary Elson of Tribune Media Services deserves thanks for adding Funny Money to the lineup of quality TMS features, as does James Lower for his patience and attention to detail in fine-tuning my weekly efforts for the syndicate.

Most of all, I want to truly thank my biggest fan and best friend, Rich Friedman, and my best-ever coworker and psychological bodyguard, Christine Tierney, for all their advice, help, encouragement, and support. Whoever wrote "Friends double our joy and divide our grief" clearly had them in mind.

This book wouldn't be possible (or necessary) without the spineless Democrats and obstructionist Republicans, Teabilly morons, lying banksters, incompetent and oblivious Treasury officials, greedy mortgage servicers, cynical corporate executives, and their obsequious lobbyists, as well as austerity-worshiping economists, ignorant Beltway deficit scolds, bond vigilantes, and, last but not least, those clueless regurgitators of failed conventional wisdom who call themselves political and economic commentators. You've all kept the American economy in such dire straits that a book about budget cutting written at the end of the Great Recessepression in 2009 is needed now more than ever, even after four years of "recovery." Really, guys, you shouldn't have.

Finally, to the working (and hoping-to-work) men and women of this country who do their best to earn a living, contribute to society, and provide for their families at a time when their own bosses, bankers, government servants, and elected representatives are doing everything in their power to make you feel just that much more scared and poor every day, I hope this book helps a little.

A note about late talkers: I've mentioned that my son is a "late talker," which refers to a child who initially shows limited vocabulary development at eighteen to thirty months old, despite being intelligent, responsive, engaged, and otherwise typical. There can be a lot of reasons for this, and most late-talking kids will eventually catch up in their language if they get the right help. They often are misdiagnosed as autistic, and they can demonstrate some autistic-looking behaviors in their attempts to navigate the world with their limited language. Autism programs are the wrong way to remedy late talking in children who aren't autistic and can actually make the situation much worse. If you suspect late talking is an issue for your child, visit the Late Talkers Foundation online,[1] contact the Natural Late Talkers support group,[2] and consult an experienced speech pathologist. It's also helpful to read *The Einstein Syndrome: Bright Children Who Talk Late* and *Late-Talking Children*, both by the economist Thomas Sowell.[3]

You can e-mail me at brian@funnymoneyblog.com or follow me at www.funnymoneyblog.com and on Twitter @BrianOCTweet. Let me know what advice worked for you, what didn't, and if I got anything wrong. On the blog you can find links to all of the online references mentioned in this book, plus the recipes from chapter 10. (Yes, even Aunt Frannie's Chili.)

Mrs. Funny Money and Funny Money Jr., or, as we call him, Li'l Money ('cuz that's all he leaves us), are characters entirely based on my family. This is not because I am making stuff up, but because anyone who wrote a humorous newspaper column that used the real names of his wife and son and reported their dialogue verbatim would soon find himself without a column, a family, or, more likely, both. Nonetheless, everything described in this book actually occurred, so I won't have to face a scolding from Oprah. Finally, I can't thank my wife and son enough for their patience, forbearance, understanding, and general good humor in tolerating my habit of mining our family life for material. As an author with a day job, I'd like to think I wrote this book in my spare time, but I really wrote it in my family's spare time.

No raccoons were harmed in the production of this book.

Notes

2

1. www.edmunds.com/car-leasing/3-ways-to-turn-your-lease-into-cash.html.
2. www.bankrate.com/brm/news/Financial_Literacy/fico-estimator.asp.
3. Liz Weston, *Your Credit Score, Your Money & What's at Stake (Updated Edition): How to Improve the 3-Digit Number That Shapes Your Financial Future* (FT Press, 2009).
4. www.irs.gov/uac/Qualified-Transportation-Fringe-Benefits-under-ARRA.
5. Chris Balish, *How to Live Well Without Owning a Car: Save Money, Breathe Easier, and Get More Mileage Out of Life* (Ten Speed Press, 2006).

3

1. www.salvationarmyusa.org/usn/www_usn_2.nsf/vw-search/D477340FFA
28755C8525743D0049D1EF?opendocument.

4

1. www.antennaweb.org.
2. www.lifelinesupport.org/ls.

5

1. Amy Dacyczyn, *The Complete Tightwad Gazette* (Villard, 1998).
2. www.irs.gov/Individuals/IRS-Withholding-Calculator.
3. www.statehealthfacts.org/comparetable.jsp?cat=7&ind=350.
4. www.insure.com/articles/healthinsurance/individual-health-coverage.html.
5. https://www.pparx.org.
6. www.needymeds.org.
7. http://findahealthcenter.hrsa.gov/Search_HCC.aspx.
8. www.nafcclinics.org.
9. www.mhakeystonecenter.org/patients.htm.

6

1. www.irs.gov/Businesses/Small-Businesses-&-Self-Employed/Deducting-Business-Expenses.
2. http://eitcoutreach.org/the-eic-estimator.
3. http://www.irs.gov/Individuals/Earned-Income-Tax-Credit-(EITC)----Use-the-EITC-Assistant-to-Find-Out-if-You-Should-Claim-it.
4. www.irs.gov/Individuals/Find-a-Location-for-Free-Tax-Prep.
5. www.aarp.org/applications/VMISLocator/searchTaxAideLocations.action.
6. https://www.fsafeds.com/forms/dcfsa_worksheet.pdf.
7. http://childcareaware.org/parents-and-guardians.

7

1. www.apa.org/news/press/releases/2008/09/credit-cash.aspx.
2. www.bankrate.com/finance/checking/checking-fees-record-highs-in-2012.aspx.
3. www.cuna.org/data/consumer/atm/welcome.html.
4. www.theco-opnetwork.org.
5. www.allpointnetwork.com.
6. www.star.com/locator.
7. www.moneypass.com.
8. www.sum-atm.com.
9. www.learnvest.com/2013/01/how-i-paid-off-35000-of-debt-over-lunch.

8

1. http://www1.umn.edu/news/features/2010/UR_CONTENT_183285.html.
2. http://mysteryshop.org.

9

1. www.insure.com/articles/lifeinsurance/the-mothers-day-index.html.
2. www.salary.com/mom-paycheck.
3. www.insure.com/home-insurance/agent-selection.html.
4. www.cfp.net.
5. www.insure.com/articles/lifeinsurance/get-better-life-insurance-rates.html.
6. www.disabilitycanhappen.org.
7. www.socialsecurity.gov/pubs/EN-05-10029.pdf.
8. http://publications.usa.gov/USAPubs.php?PubID=6042.
9. www.rtl.org/action_center/pdfs/DPOA.pdf.

10. http://online.wsj.com/article/SB1000142405270230362710457641023403925 8092.html#project%3DDOC110702%26articleTabs%3Dinteractive.

10

1. www.nrdc.org/living/eatingwell/files/foodwaste_2pgr.pdf.
2. www.nytimes.com/2012/09/05/dining/clams-and-pasta-a-quick-ocean-meal. html?hpw.
3. Dolly Freed, *Possum Living: How to Live Well Without a Job and with (Almost) No Money* (Tin House Books, 2010).
4. Jennifer Reese, *Make the Bread, Buy the Butter: What You Should and Shouldn't Cook from Scratch—Over 120 Recipes for the Best Homemade Foods* (Atria Books, 2011).

11

1. www.bankrate.com/calculators/index-of-mortgage-calculators.aspx.
2. www.bankrate.com/calculators/credit-score-fico-calculator.aspx.
3. www.myfico.com.
4. Liz Weston, *Your Credit Score, Your Money & What's at Stake (Updated Edition): How to Improve the 3-Digit Number that Shapes Your Financial Future* (FT Press, 2009).
5. www.fanniemae.com/loanlookup.
6. https://ww3.freddiemac.com/corporate.
7. www.hud.gov/offices/hsg/sfh/hcc/hcs.cfm.
8. www.irs.gov/Individuals/IRS-Withholding-Calculator.
9. www.occ.gov/news-issuances/consumer-advisories/2011/consumer-advisory-2011-1.html.

Acknowledgments

1. www.latetalkersconsulting.com.
2. www.naturallatetalkers.com.
3. Thomas Sowell, *The Einstein Syndrome: Bright Children Who Talk Late* (Basic Books, 2002); and Thomas Sowell, *Late-Talking Children* (Basic Books, 1998).